The Social
and Life
Skills MeNu

of related interest

Social Skills for Teenagers and Adults with Asperger Syndrome
A Practical Guide to Day-to-Day Life
Nancy J. Patrick
ISBN 978 1 84310 876 4

Planning to Learn
Creating and Using a Personal Planner with Young People on the
Autism Spectrum
Keely Harper-Hill and Stephanie Lord
ISBN 978 1 84310 561 9

Social Enjoyment Groups for Children, Teens and Young Adults
with Autism Spectrum Disorders
Guiding Toward Growth
John Merges
ISBN 978 1 84905 834 6

Social Skills Groups for Children and Adolescents with
Asperger's Syndrome
A Step-by-Step Program
Kim Kiker Painter
ISBN 978 1 84310 821 4

Assessing and Developing Communication and Thinking Skills
in People with Autism and Communication Difficulties
A Toolkit for Parents and Professionals
Kate Silver
With Autism Initiatives
ISBN 978 1 84310 352 3

The Social and Life Skills MeNu

A Skill Building Workbook for Adolescents with Autism Spectrum Disorders

Karra M. Barber

Jessica Kingsley *Publishers*
London and Philadelphia

First published in 2011
by Jessica Kingsley Publishers
116 Pentonville Road
London N1 9JB, UK
and
400 Market Street, Suite 400
Philadelphia, PA 19106, USA

www.jkp.com

Copyright © Karra M. Barber 2011

Library of Congress Cataloging in Publication Data
A CIP catalog record for this book is available from the Library of Congress

British Library Cataloguing in Publication Data
A CIP catalogue record for this book is available from the British Library

ISBN 978 1 84905 8 612

Printed and bound in Great Britain

Thomas — You inspire
me every day.
Scott Wada — Thank you for
your never-ending support
and encouragement.

Contents

Note: All worksheets are shown in italics below.

Author's Note

As a parent raising a child diagnosed with Asperger's syndrome, I often asked myself: if something were to happen to me, would my 16-year-old son have the ability or skill set to survive independently in the world? Does he have the social skills to convey his thoughts, feelings, and needs to the people around him and others in the community? Would he ever initiate an outing with a friend or participate socially in an organized community event?

And what about the rudimentary day-to-day living tasks? Could he manage his own bank account, budget his finances, or handle his monthly expenses appropriately? Would he know how to wash his own clothes, how to schedule a doctor's appointment, or when to get a haircut? Would he have good time-management skills or know how to multitask? I wasn't sure. Nor was I convinced that he could coordinate buying groceries with the preparation of a meal, or invite a friend over to share it with him.

And as he gets older, what about the more socially uncomfortable tasks such as returning an item to a store without a receipt, negotiating a bid for a household repair, or refuting a charge on a credit card bill? Could he do those things? If left to his own devices, I wondered if my teenage son could successfully utilize public transportation—for example, purchase a bus, plane, or train ticket, and then reach his destination without difficulty. What about safety? Would he be knowledgeable enough about how to elicit emergency services if needed? Would he know *when* they were needed? If he became lost, misguided, or confused, would he know how to approach someone for assistance? This list goes on and on…and on!

Finally, when I realized how many of these social communication skills and community life skills hadn't been practiced to the point of proficiency for my own son, it made me consider how many others like him were as unprepared for the future. This became the impetus for this book, *The Social and Life Skills MeNu: A Skill Building Workbook for Adolescents with Autism Spectrum Disorders*.

Adolescence is a time when social status is defined among peer groups. For adolescent students with a social cognitive deficit such as Asperger's syndrome or high-functioning autism, social communication skills and successful personal connections with peers are extremely difficult to develop and maintain. Whereas social conversations occur naturally among typically developing peers, for those adolescents or young adults with social cognitive deficits who lack an innate social

— 11

awareness, social exchanges are often limited and therefore need to be carefully learned.

Using a play on words, "Me and You—MeNu", *The Social and Life Skills MeNu* addresses the fact that most social conversations develop between two people. This unique workbook offers one-to-one strategies to improve self-awareness, social understanding, and basic communication skills when interacting with others in everyday life. By practicing the practical and pragmatic techniques in the MeNu workbook, students will acquire the skill set to manage effectively their social interactions with others while simultaneously developing their daily life skills in the community.

Often social conversations are shared and enjoyed at social gatherings with family, friends, and acquaintances. Whether students are socializing with friends or regularly interacting with those in the community through their daily tasks, by using the strategies outlined in this workbook, students will broaden their social experiences and independent life skills with improved self-awareness and renewed self-confidence.

What's Inside this Workbook?

Social scenarios provide a basic understanding about how people interact socially. By studying the progression of hypothetical situations in *The Social and Life Skills MeNu*, students will observe, develop, and actively engage in social scenarios of everyday living. Through practice and experiential tasks, students will improve their ability to anticipate their reactions to future social situations. Ultimately, by combining structured communication techniques, scaffolded life skill activities, and socialized community experiences, students will achieve social independence.

Education section

The Social and Life Skills MeNu uses interactive methods to examine basic functioning levels of social awareness, while providing the student and instructor with a platform to explore the social understanding of each hypothetical scenario as it applies to them. By using structured communication techniques such as interactive discussion notes and templates, students will identify alternative perspectives of effective social exchanges at various stages using four key concepts: **Prepare**, **Project**, **Practice**, and **Produce** effective communication.

Just as there are three main parts of a restaurant MeNu, similarly there are three main parts to a conversation. With that in mind, using the MeNu workbook as a template, students are guided through how to engage in social exchanges beginning with STARTER statements, moving through MAIN COURSE statements or questions, and ending with TREAT statements. The objective is for students to improve their ability to start a conversation, convey the purpose of the interaction, and end their conversation appropriately.

Implementation section

This section illustrates practical and pragmatic examples of social interplay in a variety of settings and situations. Using the four basic social skill concepts, students will enhance their social understanding and community independence. By applying life skills activities with social community experiences, students will develop a MeNu of skills from which to build their social and community tool set. The goal is to learn how to engage appropriately in social conversation with others in the community while learning independent life skills.

Four core concepts were designed to improve social communication:

- **prepare** to communicate socially

- **project** your thoughts, feelings, and ideas appropriately

- **practice** your social exchanges with others frequently

- **produce** an effective level of communication.

Chapter 1

MeNu Scenarios

Prepare to communicate socially

In this chapter: Social communication and problem solving

- Prepare to communicate socially
  - Introductory questionnaire
  - Student–instructor feedback sheet: Introductory questionnaire
  - Discussion questions: Introductory questionnaire
- Problem-solving social situations
  - Social scenario questionnaire 1
  - Student–instructor feedback sheet: Social scenario questionnaire 1
  - Discussion questions: Social scenario questionnaire 1
- Food for thought
- MeNu templates 1–10
- Chapter 1 summary

Goal

In this chapter students will identify their level of proficiency in social communication.

Objective

To prepare theoretical social responses or reactions to social situations.

> Four core concepts to improve social communication:
> - **prepare** to communicate socially
> - **project** your thoughts, feelings, and ideas appropriately
> - **practice** your social exchanges with others frequently
> - **produce** an effective level of communication.

Prepare to communicate socially
Introductory questionnaire

There are 20 questions in this section. Select answers that best describe you or how you would react in the given situations. You may select "other" to create your own answer for each question.

1. When you are communicating a specific want or need to someone else, you:

    a. are always effective

    b. are often effective

    c. are occasionally effective

    d. are never effective

    e. other: _____

2. When someone is talking to you directly, you:

    a. listen intently

    b. listen, but are occasionally distracted

    c. listen, but are often distracted

    d. don't listen at all

    e. other: _____

3. How would describe your ability to communicate verbally?

    a. consistently effective

    b. often effective

    c. occasionally successful

    d. never successful

    e. other: _____

4. How would you describe yourself at a social gathering?

    a. bold and outgoing

    b. socially comfortable

    c. a curious observer

d. shy and introverted

e. other: _____

5. When a person is explaining something important to you, but you don't understand all of the information, you:

a. ask them to clarify only the part you are unclear about

b. ask them to repeat all of the information again

c. need clarification, but say nothing

d. have a meltdown, but do not explain why

e. other: _____

6. How would your best friend describe you at a party?

a. confident and talkative

b. confident and quiet

c. quiet and awkward

d. quiet and anxious

e. other: _____

7. When you are extremely upset about something that happened at school and you want to discuss the situation, you:

a. immediately confide in a friend

b. discuss the situation with your parents right away

c. promptly announce to everyone around you what is upsetting you

d. never discuss the situation with anyone

e. other: _____

8. How well do you express yourself?

a. very well

b. pretty well

c. occasionally well

d. I have trouble expressing myself

e. other: _____

9. How would your favorite teacher describe you in a class of your peers?

    a. comfortable working in any situation

    b. comfortable when engaging with others you know well

    c. comfortable only when working alone

    d. generally anxious when working alone or with anyone

    e. other: _____

10. How would you describe yourself when you are distressed?

    a. quietly tearful

    b. quietly troubled

    c. same as always

    d. unable to contain your emotions

    e. other: _____

11. How do you think you appear when you meet someone for the first time?

    a. friendly

    b. approachable

    c. disinterested

    d. unfriendly

    e. other: _____

12. What are you most afraid of when socializing in a group of strangers?

    a. not knowing what to say

    b. not knowing what to do

    c. not knowing what they will say

    d. not knowing what they will do

    e. other: _____

13. What would upset you more?

    a. losing your pet

    b. losing your homework

    c. losing a dollar bill

    d. losing your lucky pencil

    e. other: _____

14. When a friend is angry with you about something, how would you react to them? You:

    a. would confront them and the situation calmly

    b. would confront them and the situation cautiously

    c. would confront them and the situation anxiously

    d. would not address them or the situation at all

    e. other: _____

15. How would you generally describe yourself when you are happy?

    a. excited

    b. bubbly

    c. cheerful

    d. same as always

    e. other: _____

16. How would you generally describe yourself when you are sad?

    a. tearful

    b. sullen

    c. miserable

    d. the same as always

    e. other: _____

17. When you meet someone new and would like to get to know them better, you:

    a. talk to them

    b. observe them

    c. ignore them

    d. do nothing

    e. other: _____

18. What are your best social skills?

    a. listening while participating in a conversation

    b. listening while reading subtle non-verbal cues

    c. listening while using occasional eye contact

   d.　I don't have a "best" social skill

   e.　other: _____

19. What do you think your parents would say about your ability to interact socially?

   a.　always proficient

   b.　often proficient

   c.　occasionally proficient

   d.　rarely proficient

   e.　other: _____

20. How would you describe yourself when you interact with people in the community?

   a.　often capable

   b.　often shy, but proficient

   c.　often uneasy, but effective

   d.　often introverted and not effective

   e.　other: _____

Interpreting your questionnaire answers

Total your score. How many a, b, c, d, or e answers did you have? Add the total for each. There are no wrong answers. Information from this exercise reveals your current level of ability in social communication. Collectively, answers may vary based on your age, developmental level, or social cognitive ability.

a_____ proficient

b_____ requires practice

c_____ needs assistance

d_____ challenged

e_____ other

The information in this questionnaire answer key is only to be used as a student guide.

Prepare to communicate socially
Student–instructor feedback sheet: Introductory questionnaire

Questionnaire feedback worksheets are used as a method to discuss further each questionnaire answer with your instructor. Please explain and discuss your questionnaire answers with your instructor.

What were your answers to each of these questions and why? Please explain.

1. When you are communicating a specific want or need to someone else, you:

   _____

   _____

   _____

2. When someone is talking to you directly, you: _____

   _____

   _____

   _____

3. How would describe your ability to communicate verbally?_____

   _____

   _____

   _____

4. How would you describe yourself at a social gathering? _____

   _____

   _____

   _____

5. When a person is explaining something important to you, but you don't understand all of the information, you: _____

   _____

   _____

   _____

6. How would your best friend describe you at a party? _____

_____

_____

_____

7. When you are extremely upset about something that happened at school and you want to discuss the situation, you: _____

_____

_____

_____

8. How well do you express yourself? _____

_____

_____

_____

9. How would your favorite teacher describe you in a class of your peers? _____

_____

_____

_____

10. How would you describe yourself when you are distressed? _____

_____

_____

_____

11. How do you think you appear when you meet someone for the first time? _____

_____

_____

_____

12. What are you most afraid of when socializing in a group of strangers? _____

_____

_____

_____

13. What would upset you more—losing your pet, losing your homework, losing a dollar bill, losing your lucky pencil, or other? _____

_____

_____

_____

14. When a friend is angry with you about something, how would you react to them? _____

_____

_____

_____

15. How would you generally describe yourself when you are happy? _____

_____

_____

_____

16. How would you generally describe yourself when you are sad? _____

_____

_____

_____

17. When you meet someone new and would like to get to know them better, you:

_____

_____

_____

18. What are your best social skills? _____

_____

_____

_____

19. What do you think your parents would say about your ability to interact socially?

_____

_____

_____

20. How would you describe yourself when you interact with people in the community? _____

_____

_____

_____

Prepare to communicate socially
Discussion questions: Introductory questionnaire

Review each questionnaire answer with your instructor and answer the following questions:

• How do you feel about socially communicating with others?

_____

_____

_____

_____

• Did you discover anything new about yourself from this exercise?

_____

_____

_____

• Did any of your answers surprise you?

_____

_____

_____

• What particular areas of social communication would you like to improve upon?

_____

_____

_____

_____

• Did you find this exercise useful? Why or why not?

_____

_____

_____

_____

Problem-solving social situations
Social scenario questionnaire 1

There are 20 questions in this section. Select answers that best describe how you think you would react in the social scenarios below. You may select "other" to create your own answer.

1. A friend calls one afternoon and invites you to dinner at their house that evening, but you're in the middle of doing your homework when they call. You:

   a. politely turn down the invitation and finish your homework

   b. kindly tell them that you will get back to them shortly, while you check with your parents

   c. immediately stop what you are doing and tell them that you'll be right over

   d. become anxious because you can't decide what to do

   e. other: _____

   _____

   _____

2. You are the new student at your high school and have trouble making friends easily. You:

   a. join a club to meet other students with common interests

   b. introduce yourself to other students, despite your discomfort

   c. wait until another student initiates a friendship with you

   d. do nothing

   e. other: _____

   _____

   _____

3. You are tired of eating lunch alone every day at school. You:

    a. offer to share your lunch with someone so they will spend time with you

    b. approach a classmate(s) that you know and hint that you'd like to join them

    c. skip eating lunch all together

    d. feel bad, but make no effort to change your situation

    e. other: _____

_____

_____

4. Your partner in chemistry lab never does their share of the lab work and this bothers you. You:

    a. ask your chemistry partner to pitch in more

    b. immediately explain the situation to the teacher and ask for their help

    c. survey the other students to find a new chemistry partner

    d. do nothing

    e. other: _____

_____

_____

5. You agree to meet a teammate at the local pizzeria after your soccer game, but you lose track of time. You arrive 30 minutes late and your teammate is no longer there. You:

    a. call your teammate to apologize and ask if they can still meet you at the pizzeria

    b. leave the pizzeria and apologize to your teammate the next day

    c. do nothing because you don't know what to do

    d. assume your teammate forgot to meet you at the pizzeria

    e. other: _____

_____

_____

6. Some students in your P.E. class are making negative remarks about your athletic ability during class. You:

   a. politely ask them to stop

   b. ignore their comments

   c. get upset and tell the P.E. coach

   d. tell your parents you no longer want to take P.E. class

   e. other: _____

   _____

   _____

7. You and your little sister are home alone and you decide to cook something on the stove for dinner. Suddenly you smell something burning from your kitchen, but you don't see any smoke and can't determine the source. You:

   a. turn off the stove immediately and call the fire department to explain the situation

   b. turn off the stove, exit your house immediately (with your sister), and wait for your parents to come home

   c. do nothing since you don't see any smoke coming from the stove

   d. instantly become alarmed and hysterically call your parent(s)

   e. other: _____

   _____

   _____

8. You have an A+ grade in English class, but missed the final test because you were out sick on the day it was given. You:

   a. ask your teacher if your missed test will affect your grade

   b. are worried about your perfect grade and ask your teacher if you can take a make-up exam

   c. do nothing because you don't know what to do

   d. do nothing because you don't care

   e. other: _____

   _____

   _____

9. You have a friend over to your house after school and decide to make cookies for the school fundraiser. Your friend would rather make a cake than cookies, and you can't seem to agree. You:

   a. compromise and decide to make both

   b. concede and make the cake instead

   c. tell your friend you are making cookies and it's not negotiable

   d. get upset and ask your friend to leave

   e. other: _____

   _____

   _____

10. You're out to lunch with a friend from school when you realize that you have forgotten your lunch money. You:

    a. tell your friend that you've forgotten your money and ask if they have any money to loan you

    b. tell your friend that you've forgotten your money and ask if they will share their lunch with you

    c. say nothing and eat nothing

    d. ask if you can have your friend's lunch to eat

    e. other: _____

    _____

    _____

11. You and a friend are reprimanded for talking in class, but only you get detention for it, and this upsets you. You:

    a. explain to the teacher why you feel the punishment isn't fair

    b. expect your friend to accept responsibility too

    c. say nothing and assume the punishment alone

    d. get upset with your friend and the teacher

    e. other: _____

    _____

    _____

12. You're at a restaurant with your sister and you've both ordered your meal. But when your meal arrives, it's not exactly how you've ordered it. You:

    a. politely explain why you must return your meal and ask for it to be corrected

    b. express your disappointment to your server and ask for other options

    c. refuse to eat your meal and pout until your sister finishes her meal

    d. abruptly leave the restaurant and threaten never to return

    e. other: _____

    _____

    _____

13. You witnessed a student rear-end a vacant car in the school parking lot. You:

    a. immediately tell the school principal what you witnessed

    b. assume the student involved will handle the situation

    c. say nothing unless someone asks for your input

    d. call the police immediately and report the incident

    e. other: _____

    _____

    _____

14. You're a guest at your cousin's graduation party. It's a sit-down dinner and you quickly realize that nothing the host is serving is anything you ordinarily eat. You:

    a. compliment the host, but politely explain that you have dietary issues and unfortunately can't eat the meal

    b. decide to taste a few of the dishes anyway

    c. fake a stomach ache and asked to be excused

    d. announce to everyone at the table that the menu is ridiculous

    e. other: _____

    _____

    _____

15. You want to learn how to drive a car, but your parents don't think you are ready. You disagree. You:

   a. decide to study for the driver's license test to prove to them you are ready

   b. are upset, but understand your parents' concerns

   c. nag your parents until they give in

   d. practice driving illegally, despite your parents' concerns

   e. other: _____

_____

_____

16. You and a group of your school friends meet before school for breakfast. The server brings you your meal first, while everyone else at your table is still waiting to be served. You:

   a. wait until the entire group is served and then eat yours

   b. ask the others at the table if they mind if you start eating before them

   c. Start eating because you are hungry

   d. wait for the next guest to get their food and then eat yours

   e. other: _____

_____

_____

17. You've wanted to play the drums in the school band for over a year, but you are nervous because you have sensory issues. When you finally have enough courage to join, your music teacher tells you she doesn't think it's a good idea. You:

   a. attend a few band practices and see how it affects you

   b. join anyway, despite your concerns and your teacher's warning

   c. take her word for it and decide to join a different school club

   d. realize it was a bad idea, but decide to play a different instrument

   e. other: _____

_____

_____

18. Your brother's friend is at your house having a meal with you and your family. You notice that your brother's friend is chewing with his mouth open, licking his fingers, and wiping his mouth with his shirt sleeve instead of using his napkin. You:

   a. offer your brother's friend a napkin

   b. pretend not to notice him

   c. are embarrassed and tell your brother's friend he's rude

   d. leave the table in disgust

   e. other: _____

   _____

   _____

19. You discover your friend is taking prescription medication that is not prescribed for them and you are concerned. You:

   a. tell their parents

   b. tell your parents

   c. explain your concerns to them

   d. do nothing

   e. other: _____

   _____

   _____

20. You just found out that your best friend is moving across town and won't be attending your high school anymore. You:

   a. are upset, but understand

   b. recognize that situations change, but plan to keep in touch

   c. are inconsolable and can't imagine school the same without them

   d. look for a new best friend

   e. other: _____

   _____

   _____

Interpreting your questionnaire answers

Total your score. How many a, b, c, d, or e answers did you have? Add the total for each. There are no wrong answers. Information from this exercise reveals your current level of ability to problem-solve in a social context from the scenarios provided. Collectively, answers may vary based on your age, developmental level, and social cognitive ability.

a_____ proficient

b_____ requires practice

c_____ needs assistance

d_____ challenged

e_____ other

The information in this questionnaire answer key is only to be used as a student guide.

Problem-solving social situations
Student–instructor feedback sheet: Social scenario questionnaire 1

Questionnaire feedback worksheets are used as a method to discuss further each questionnaire answer with your instructor. Explain *how* you problem-solved each scenario. What was your reasoning?

What were your answers to each of these questions and why? Explain.

1. A friend calls one afternoon and invites you to dinner at their house that evening, but you're in the middle of doing your homework when they call. You:_____

    _____

    _____

    _____

2. You are the new student at your high school and have trouble making friends easily. You: _____

    _____

    _____

    _____

3. You are tired of eating lunch alone every day at school. You: _____

    _____

    _____

    _____

4. Your partner in chemistry lab never does their share of the lab work and this bothers you. You: _____

    _____

    _____

    _____

5. You agree to meet a teammate at the local pizzeria after your soccer game, but you lose track of time. You arrive 30 minutes late and your teammate is no longer there. You:_____

_____

_____

_____

6. Some students in your P.E. class are making negative remarks about your athletic ability during class. You: _____

_____

_____

_____

7. You and your little sister are home alone and you decide to cook something on the stove for dinner. Suddenly you smell something burning from your kitchen, but you don't see any smoke and can't determine the source. You: _____

_____

_____

_____

8. You have an A+ grade in English class, but missed the final test because you were out sick the day it was given. You:_____

_____

_____

_____

9. You have a friend over to your house after school and decide to make cookies for the school fundraiser. Your friend would rather make a cake than cookies, and you can't seem to agree. You:_____

_____

_____

_____

10. You're out to lunch with a friend from school when you realize that you have forgotten your lunch money. You: _____

_____

_____

_____

11. You and a friend are reprimanded for talking in class, but only you get detention for it, and this upsets you. You: _____

_____

_____

_____

12. You're at a restaurant with your sister and you've both ordered your meal. But when your meal arrives, it's not exactly how you've ordered it. You: _____

_____

_____

_____

13. You saw a student rear-end a vacant car in the school parking lot. You: _____

_____

_____

_____

14. You're a guest at your cousin's graduation party. It's a sit-down dinner and you quickly realize that nothing the host is serving is anything you ordinarily eat. You: _____

_____

_____

_____

15. You want to learn how to drive a car, but your parents don't think you are ready. You disagree. You: _____

_____

_____

_____

16. You and a group of your school friends meet before school for breakfast. The server brings you your meal first, while everyone else at your table is still waiting to be served. You: _____

_____

_____

_____

17. You've wanted to play the drums in the school band for over a year, but you are nervous because you have sensory issues. When you finally have enough courage to join, your music teacher tells you she doesn't think it's a good idea. You:___

_____

_____

_____

18. Your brother's friend is at your house having a meal with you and your family. You notice that your brother's friend is chewing with his mouth open, licking his fingers, and wiping his mouth with his shirt sleeve instead of using his napkin. You: _____

_____

_____

_____

19. You discover your friend is taking prescription medication that is not prescribed for them and you are concerned. You: _____

_____

_____

20. You just found out that your best friend is moving across town and won't be attending your high school anymore. You:_____

_____

_____

_____

Problem-solving social situations
Discussion questions: Social scenario questionnaire 1

Review each questionnaire answer with your instructor and answer the following questions:

• Which social situation could you identify with best?

_____

_____

_____

_____

• Do you feel that you have good problem-solving skills?

_____

_____

_____

_____

• What questions were most relevant to you and the way you communicate?

_____

_____

_____

_____

• What did you learn most about yourself from this exercise?

_____

_____

_____

_____

- How would you prepare yourself to problem-solve in a social setting in the future?

_____

_____

_____

- How do these social scenarios compare to your real-life personal experiences?

_____

_____

_____

- How did you score on the problem-solving questionnaire?

_____

_____

_____

- Is there an area you feel you could improve?

_____

_____

_____

Food for thought

Think of the MeNu as a social reference on how to:

- Start a conversation
- Convey the purpose of your conversation
- End the conversation.

Review the following MeNu template examples describing various social scenarios.

Using the MeNu template examples as a social reference, complete templates creating your own social dialogue for each starter, main course, and treat.

Good social communication details
MeNu template example 1

Social scenario

You arrive late at the Burger Hut restaurant when meeting a friend for lunch. This is an example of your conversation with the hostess.

Starter

(Start a conversation with an introduction statement)

> You: "Hi, my name is (insert your name)"

> Restaurant Host: "Hello."

Main course

(Convey the purpose of your conversation with a statement and/or question)

> You: "I'm supposed to meet my friend Beth Smith here for lunch at noon, but I'm late. Do you know if she's already been seated at a table?"

> Restaurant Host: "Yes, she has. Let me take you to her table."

Treat

(End the conversation with a statement)

> You: "Thanks so much for your help."

Good social communication details
Student MeNu template 1a

Using the MeNu template in the last example as reference, read the same social scenario below and create your own social conversation.

Social scenario

You arrive late at the Burger Hut restaurant when meeting a friend for lunch.

Starter

(Start a conversation with an introduction statement)

_____

_____

Main course

(Convey the purpose of your conversation with a statement and/or question)

_____

_____

_____

_____

Treat

(End the conversation with a statement)

_____

_____

Lacking social communication details
MeNu template example 2

The scenario on this page is an example of the *wrong* way to go about this conversation. Think about how the person you're communicating with might feel.

Social scenario

You arrive late at the Burger Hut restaurant when meeting a friend for lunch. This is an example of your conversation with the host.

Starter

(Start a conversation with an introduction statement)

> You: "Hi."
>
> Restaurant Host: "Hi. What do you need?"

Main course

(Convey the purpose of your conversation with a statement and/or question)

> You: "Oh, I'm supposed to meet my friend here for lunch. Do you know if she's here yet?"
>
> Restaurant Host: "How would I know? Who is your friend?"
>
> You: "Oh. Her name is Beth."
>
> Restaurant Host: "What's her last name?"
>
> You: "Smith."
>
> Restaurant Host: "No, I don't think she's here."
>
> You: "How do you know for sure?"
>
> Restaurant Host: "I just looked at my reservation book and I don't see that she's checked in!"

Treat

(End the conversation with a statement)

> You: "Oh. Then I think I'll just wait until I see her."
>
> Restaurant Host: "Whatever!"

Lacking social communication details
Student MeNu template example 2a

Using the MeNu template in the last example as reference, read the same social scenario below and create your own social conversation.

Social scenario

You arrive late at the Burger Hut restaurant when meeting a friend for lunch.

Starter

(Start a conversation with an introduction statement)

_____

_____

Main course

(Convey the purpose of your conversation with a statement and/or question)

_____

_____

_____

_____

Treat

(End the conversation with a statement)

_____

_____

Appropriately persistent
MeNu template example 3

Social scenario

You want to study for an upcoming science test with your classmate, Molly. She sits behind you in class, and, like you, science is one of her favorite subjects in school. How do you ask Molly if she'd like to study with you?

Starter

(Start a conversation with an introduction statement)

> You: "Hi Molly! Are you ready for the science test next week?"

> Molly: "Not yet, but I will be soon."

Main course

(Convey the purpose of your conversation with a statement and/or question)

> You: "I was wondering if you'd like to study for the test together this weekend. I recorded all the chapter notes and got an A on the last science quiz. I know we both like science and I thought we'd be good study partners."

> Molly: "Yes, that sounds like a great idea. Can you meet me next Saturday morning at the library right when it opens?"

Treat

(End the conversation with a statement)

> You: "Yes. I can meet you at the library Saturday morning. It opens at 10 a.m. I'll see you then, Molly."

> Molly: "OK. I will see you then."

Appropriately persistent
Student MeNu template example 3a

Using the MeNu template in the last example as reference, read the same social scenario below and create your own social conversation.

Social scenario

You want to study for an upcoming science test with your classmate, Molly. She sits behind you in class, and, like you, science is one of her favorite subjects in school. How do you ask Molly if she'd like to study with you?

Starter

(Start a conversation with an introduction statement)

_____

_____

Main course

(Convey the purpose of your conversation with a statement and/or question)

_____

_____

_____

_____

Treat

(End the conversation with a statement)

_____

_____

Overly persistent
MeNu template example 4

The scenario on this page is an example of the *wrong* way to go about this conversation. Think about how the person you're communicating with might feel.

Social scenario

You want to study for an upcoming science test with your classmate, Molly. She sits behind you in class, and, like you, science is one of her favorite subjects in school. How do you ask Molly if she'd like to study with you?

Starter

(Start a conversation with an introduction statement)

> You: "Hi Molly! Are you ready for the science test next week?"
>
> Molly: "Um, I guess."

Main course

(Convey the purpose of your conversation with a statement and/or question)

> You: "I really want us to study together this weekend. My science notes are very organized and complete, and I know we both like science, so it makes perfect sense for us to study together."
>
> Molly: "Um, I'm cool studying on my own, but thanks."
>
> You: "Oh. But I can meet you at the library Saturday morning so we can study together. It's no trouble. It opens at 10 a.m., and…"
>
> Molly: "Um, I'm going to study on my own, OK. Besides, I don't really know you that well."
>
> You: "Oh, are you sure? Because I can meet you…"
>
> Molly: "YES, I'M SURE! Please don't ask me again."

Treat

(End the conversation with a statement)

> You: "OK."
>
> Molly: "BYE!"

Overly persistent
Student MeNu template example 4a

Using the MeNu template in the last example as reference, read the same social scenario below and create your own social conversation.

Social scenario

You want to study for an upcoming science test with your classmate, Molly. She sits behind you in class, and, like you, science is one of her favorite subjects in school. How do you ask Molly if she'd like to study with you?

Starter

(Start a conversation with an introduction statement)

_____

_____

Main course

(Convey the purpose of your conversation with a statement and/or question)

_____

_____

_____

_____

Treat

(End the conversation with a statement)

_____

_____

Socially aware
MeNu template example 5

Social scenario

After rehearsing your lines together for weeks, you and your best friend both audition for the lead role in the school play. When the casting list is posted, you are ecstatic to learn you've been offered the lead role, while your best friend is devastated by the news. What do you say to your best friend without making her feel worse?

Starter

(Start a conversation with an introduction statement)

> You: "So apparently I've been given the lead role in the play."

> Friend: "Yes, I know."

Main course

(Convey the purpose of your conversation with a statement and/or question)

> You: "I'm sorry that you weren't selected for the role. I'm sure it meant a lot to you. I think you would have been great for the part too. Is there anything I can say to make you feel better?"

> Friend: "No. But thanks for asking. Congratulations."

Treat

(End the conversation with a statement)

> You: "Oh, why thank you."

Socially aware
Student MeNu template example 5a

Using the MeNu template in the last example as reference, read the same social scenario below and create your own social conversation.

Social scenario

After rehearsing your lines together for weeks, you and your best friend both audition for the lead role in the school play. When the casting list is posted, you are ecstatic to learn you've been offered the lead role, while your best friend is devastated by the news. What do you say to your best friend without making her feel worse?

Starter

(Start a conversation with an introduction statement)

_____

_____

Main course

(Convey the purpose of your conversation with a statement and/or question)

_____

_____

_____

_____

Treat

(End the conversation with a statement)

_____

_____

Socially unaware
MeNu template example 6

The scenario on this page is an example of the *wrong* way to go about this conversation. Think about how the person you're communicating with might feel.

Social scenario

After rehearsing your lines together for weeks, you and your best friend both audition for the same role in the school play. When the casting list is posted, you are ecstatic to learn you've been offered the lead role, while your best friend is devastated by the news. What do you say to your best friend without making her feel worse?

Starter

(Start a conversation with an introduction statement)

> You: "Did you hear? I got the lead role in the play. I am *so excited*!"
>
> Friend: "Yes, I can tell."

Main course

(Convey the purpose of your conversation with a statement and/or question)

> You: "Too bad you didn't get picked for the role. But I'm *thrilled I did*! What can I say?"
>
> Friend: "If you were a real friend, you'd say you'll give me the role instead of you!"
>
> You: "Listen, I got that role fair and square. The truth is, I must have auditioned better than you. Sorry!"
>
> Friend: "You knew I wanted that part as much as you did. You are gloating and I can't believe you are so insensitive to my feelings. I don't know if I can be friends with you anymore."
>
> You: "Don't you think you're overreacting a bit?"
>
> Friend: "No! I'm very upset."

Treat

(End the conversation with a statement)

> You: "See you in drama class, I guess."
>
> Friend: "GOODBYE!"

Socially unaware
Student MeNu template example 6a

Using the MeNu template in the last example as reference, read the same social scenario below and create your own social conversation.

Social scenario

After rehearsing your lines together for weeks, you and your best friend both audition for the same role in the school play. When the casting list is posted, you are ecstatic to learn you've been offered the lead role, while your best friend is devastated by the news. What do you say to your best friend without making her feel worse?

Starter

(Start a conversation with an introduction statement)

_____

_____

Main course

(Convey the purpose of your conversation with a statement and/or question)

_____

_____

_____

_____

Treat

(End the conversation with a statement)

_____

_____

Accepting responsibility in a social setting
MeNu template example 7

Social scenario

You just got fired from your part-time job at the restaurant for accidentally breaking a few dishes and confusing several food orders. You were counting on that job to earn money toward a soccer camp. How will you tell your parents?

Starter

(Start a conversation with an introduction statement)

> You: "You're not going to believe what happened to me today!"

> Parent: "What happened?"

Main course

(Convey the purpose of your conversation with a statement and/or question)

> You: "Unfortunately, I was fired from my job. Because I broke a few dishes and messed up a few meal orders, the owner said I needed more restaurant experience. How will I earn enough money to go to soccer camp now? I'm still $75 short."

> Parent: "I can loan you the money. You can pay me back by doing extra chores."

Treat

(End the conversation with a statement)

> You: "OK, I will. I can wash the car, clean the garage, and paint the shed. Thanks, Mom."

Accepting responsibility in a social setting
Student MeNu template example 7a

Using the MeNu template in the last example as reference, read the same social scenario below and create your own social conversation.

Social scenario

You just got fired from your part-time job at the restaurant for accidentally breaking a few dishes and confusing several food orders. You were counting on that job to earn money toward a soccer camp. How will you tell your parents?

Starter

(Start a conversation with an introduction statement)

_____

_____

Main course

(Convey the purpose of your conversation with a statement and/or question)

_____

_____

_____

_____

Treat

(End the conversation with a statement)

_____

_____

Not accepting responsibility
MeNu template example 8

The scenario on this page is an example of the *wrong* way to go about this conversation. Think about how the person you're communicating with might feel.

Social scenario

You just got fired from your part-time job at the restaurant for accidentally breaking a few dishes and confusing several food orders. You were counting on that job to earn money toward a soccer camp. How will you tell your parents?

Starter

(Start a conversation with an introduction statement)

> You: "I was treated unfairly today at work!"
>
> Parent: "What happened?"

Main course

(Convey the purpose of your conversation with a statement and/or question)

> You: "I was fired from my job because I accidentally broke a few dishes and mistakenly messed up a few meal orders. Because of my 'lack of experience' the owner fired me. Now I don't have enough money to go to soccer camp. I'm still $75 short."
>
> Parent: "How do plan to earn the $75 you need?"
>
> You: "I don't know."
>
> Parent: "Me either. Maybe you can't go this year."
>
> You: "But, I go every year. That's not fair."
>
> Parent: "Well, if you don't have the money, it doesn't sound as if you can go."
>
> You: "But I was fired unfairly."
>
> Parent: "Life isn't always fair."
>
> You: "That's not fair. I still want to go to soccer camp."

Treat

(End the conversation with a statement)

> Parent: "Looks as if you will need to get another job if you want to earn the $75."
>
> You: "Ughh!"

Not accepting responsibility
Student MeNu template example 8a

Using the MeNu template in the last example as reference, read the same social scenario below and create your own social conversation.

Social scenario

You just got fired from your part-time job at the restaurant for accidentally breaking a few dishes and confusing several food orders. You were counting on that job to earn money toward a soccer camp. How will you tell your parents?

Starter

(Start a conversation with an introduction statement)

_____

_____

Main course

(Convey the purpose of your conversation with a statement and/or question)

_____

_____

_____

_____

Treat

(End the conversation with a statement)

_____

_____

Create your own social scenario dialogue
Student MeNu template 9

Social scenario

It's your final year in high school and you just got your class schedule. Although you like most of your classes, one of your classes is taught by a teacher you don't get along with. Unfortunately, it's a course you have to graduate. How will you handle this situation? Will your conversation be with your teacher, best friend, or parents?

Starter

(Start a conversation with an introduction statement)

_____

_____

Main course

(Convey the purpose of your conversation with a statement and/or question)

_____

_____

_____

_____

Treat

(End the conversation with a statement)

_____

_____

Create your own social scenario dialogue
Student MeNu template 10

Social scenario

Create a social scenario about you, a friend, and a school-related issue.

Starter

(Start a conversation with an introduction statement)

_____

_____

Main course

(Convey the purpose of your conversation with a statement and/or question)

_____

_____

_____

_____

Treat

(End the conversation with a statement)

_____

_____

Chapter 1 summary

In this chapter, strategies to improve self-awareness, social understanding, and social communication skills were addressed using interactive questionnaires and hypothetical social scenarios. Using sample topics, students identified, evaluated, and problem-solved social situations using MeNu interactive templates. Student–instructor feedback was used to review, record, and discuss chapter content.

Goal

In this chapter students identified their level of proficiency in social communication examples.

Objective

To prepare theoretical social responses or reactions to social situations.

Starter MeNu Topics

Project your thoughts, feelings, and ideas appropriately

In this chapter: Identifying perspectives and topic planning

- Project your thoughts, feelings, and ideas appropriately
  - Social scenario questionnaire 2: Identifying perspectives
  - Student–instructor feedback sheet: Social scenario questionnaire 2
  - Discussion questions: Social scenario questionnaire 2
  - True or false questionnaire
  - Student–instructor feedback sheet: True or false questionnaire
- Topic planning MeNu principles
  - Starters
  - Main course
  - Treats
- Practice using the social MeNu
  - Social dialogue: Family barbecue
  - Social dialogue: Lunch break with a peer at school
- Topic planning activities 1–4
- Topic planning discussion questions
- Chapter 2 summary

Goal

In this chapter students will examine how to project their thoughts, feelings, and ideas appropriately while identifying the perspectives of others in various social interactions.

Objective

Using topic examples from MeNu principles, to understand the concept of topic planning. Students will implement their ideas and interests as these relate to a topic of conversation in the prescribed exercises outlined in this chapter.

Four core concepts to improve social communication:

- **prepare** to communicate socially

- **project** your thoughts, feelings, and ideas appropriately

- **practice** your social exchanges with others frequently

- **produce** an effective level of communication.

Project your thoughts, feelings, and ideas appropriately
Social scenario questionnaire 2: Identifying perspectives

There are ten questions in this section. Select answers that best describe how you think you would react in the social scenarios below. You may select "other" to create your own answer.

1. You and a friend are discussing a controversial topic. You notice your friend getting upset when they realize that you don't hold the same opinion as them. You:

    a. acknowledge that your friend is upset by the difference in opinions and offer to change the subject when there is a pause

    b. tell your friend that you agree to disagree and eventually change the topic

    c. are tired of the conversation topic and walk away while your friend is still talking

    d. End the conversation abruptly

    e. other: _____

2. You're at a family party and one of your uncles is telling a story to a group at the party. You disagree with the "facts" in his story. You:

    a. recognize that your uncle may be embellishing the facts of his story to make it more interesting, but you do not correct him

    b. pull your uncle aside privately and correct him on his story

    c. politely excuse yourself from the group and take a break

    d. announce to everyone at the party your uncle is not truthful

    e. other: _____

3. A girl in class invites you over to celebrate her Hawaiian-themed birthday party. She really wants you to come, but you don't like Hawaiian foods and you won't know many of the other guests invited. This makes you anxious. You:

    a. agree to attend the party knowing that you may feel anxious some of the time

b. attend the party, but ask the birthday girl to introduce you to the party guests you don't know

c. attend the party, try the Hawaiian food, but avoid all of the guests you don't know

d. decline the invitation and stay home alone because you think you'll be uncomfortable at the party

e. other: _____

4. You and your family are having dinner around the table. Everyone is chatting, except for you. Noticing your silence, your mother engages you directly in the family conversation with questions. You:

a. take the hint that you should engage in the conversation and ask other family members questions too

b. answer your mother's questions, eventually commenting on the ongoing group conversation

c. answer your mother's questions with yes or no answers

d. sit quietly until someone finally discusses a topic that is of interest to you

e. other: _____

5. You are eating dinner at a friend's house one evening with a group of their friends. You quickly find yourself involved in a religious debate among the other dinner guests, and the discussion becomes heated. You have strong religious beliefs and want to share your opinion. You:

a. listen intently and speak freely with the understanding that everyone's entitled to their own opinion without judgment

b. realize the topic is controversial and carefully decide how you will share your opinion with others

c. argue your point until the others acquiesce

d. can't handle the emerging conflict and leave the table distraught

e. other: _____

6. You are invited to your relative's cabin for a holiday with other extended family members. You are expected to attend, but you aren't comfortable socializing in such a large group of your relatives. You:

   a. realize that you won't be comfortable, but attend anyway, knowing your relatives would enjoy socializing with you

   b. attend because you understand it's an opportunity to practice your social skills with your relatives

   c. attend, but do not engage much at all with your relatives

   d. stay home because the group is too large to interact with

   e. other: _____

7. You are in the middle of telling a funny story to a friend and another friend keeps interrupting your story and changing the subject. This bothers you. You:

   a. continue telling your story and ignore the friend that is interrupting you

   b. politely ask the friend to stop interrupting you

   c. assume the story is not important to either friend and stop telling it all together

   d. get annoyed, stop talking, and walk away abruptly

   e. other: _____

8. Your best friend is extremely quiet; they rarely initiate a conversation with you, and you are tired of doing most of the talking. You:

   a. tell them you'd like to have a more "shared" conversation and ask them if prompting them with open-ended questions would be helpful

   b. accept their "shyness" and try and engage in conversations on topics that are interesting to them

   c. decide to accept less interactive conversations with them

   d. decide to stop talking to them all together

   e. other: _____

9. You are at a social event and overhear someone say some things about you that are untrue, and this upsets you. You:

    a. approach the person immediately and correct them on what you overheard

    b. assume they are misinformed and decide not to react at all

    c. get angry and yell at the person for spreading untruths

    d. leave the party upset

    e. other: _____

10. You are involved in a discussion about a current event with a few people at a social gathering, but you become bored with the topic of conversation. You try and change the subject, but the original topic keeps resurfacing. You:

    a. pretend to be interested in the topic and continue to listen intently

    b. decide to listen longer to determine what others find so fascinating about the topic being discussed

    c. can't believe people are interested in talking about a topic you find irrelevant

    d. announce that you need to find a more interesting group of people to talk to

    e. other: _____

Interpreting your questionnaire answers

Total your score. How many a, b, c, d, or e answers did you have? Add the total for each. There are no wrong answers. Information from this exercise reveals your current level of ability to identify perspectives in a social context. Collectively, answers may vary based on your age, developmental level, and social cognitive ability.

a_____ proficient

b_____ requires practice

c_____ needs assistance

d_____ challenged

e_____ other

The information in this questionnaire answer key is only to be used as a student guide.

Project your thoughts, feelings, and ideas appropriately
Student–instructor feedback sheet: Social scenario questionnaire 2

Questionnaire feedback worksheets are used as a method to discuss further each questionnaire answer with your instructor. Please explain *how* you identified with various perspectives in each scenario. What was your reasoning? What situations could you relate to best?

What were your answers to each of these questions and why? Explain.

1. You and a friend are discussing a controversial topic. You notice your friend getting upset when they realize that you don't hold the same opinion as them. You: _____

_____

_____

_____

2. You're at a family party and one of your uncles is telling a story to a group at the party. You disagree with the "facts" in his story. You: _____

_____

_____

_____

3. A girl in class invites you over to celebrate her Hawaiian-themed birthday party. She really wants you to come, but you don't like Hawaiian foods and you won't know many of the other guests invited. This makes you anxious. You: _____

_____

_____

_____

4. You and your family are having dinner around the table. Everyone is chatting, except for you. Noticing your silence, your mother engages you directly in the family conversation with questions. You: _____

_____

_____

_____

5. You are eating dinner at a friend's house one evening with a group of their friends. You quickly find yourself involved in a religious debate among the other dinner guests, and the discussion becomes heated. You have strong religious beliefs and want to share your opinion. You: _____

_____

_____

_____

6. You are invited to your relative's cabin for a holiday with other extended family members. You are expected to attend, but you aren't comfortable socializing in such a large group of your relatives. You: _____

_____

_____

_____

7. You are in the middle of telling a funny story to a friend and another friend keeps interrupting your story and changing the subject. This bothers you. You:

_____

_____

_____

8. Your best friend is extremely quiet; they rarely initiate a conversation with you, and you are tired of doing most of the talking. You:_____

_____

_____

_____

9. You are at a social event and overhear someone say some things about you that are untrue, and this upsets you. You: _____

_____

_____

_____

10. You are involved in a discussion about a current event with a few people at a social gathering, but you become bored with the topic of conversation. You try and change the subject, but the original topic keeps resurfacing. You: _____

_____

_____

_____

Project your thoughts, feelings, and ideas appropriately

Discussion questions: Social scenario questionnaire 2

Review each questionnaire answer with your instructor and answer the following questions:

- How did you identify with perspective taking in the questionnaire social scenarios?

_____

_____

_____

_____

- Which social scenario did you relate to the best? Please explain.

_____

_____

_____

_____

- Did you discover anything new about yourself from this exercise? Please explain.

_____

_____

_____

_____

- Did any of your answers surprise you? How so?

_____

_____

_____

_____

- What particular areas of social communication would you like to improve upon?

_____

_____

_____

_____

- Do you feel more aware of other people's perspectives after completing this exercise? Why or why not? Give an example.

_____

_____

_____

_____

Project your thoughts, feelings, and ideas appropriately
True or false questionnaire

This questionnaire will help you to identify your current level of self-awareness in a social context. There are 20 true or false questions in this section. Please select an answer that best describes you, marking **T** for true or **F** for false for each question.

1. I feel relaxed at school or at social gatherings. _____

2. I feel comfortable when interacting with my friends. _____

3. It's easy for me to talk to someone I don't know. _____

4. My peers perceive me as friendly and sociable. _____

5. I have good eye contact when talking to people in general. _____

6. I feel comfortable sharing my thoughts with my peer group. _____

7. I can appreciate someone else's perspective even when I don't agree with them. _____

8. I understand innuendos and inferences in a general conversation. _____

9. I can easily read someone else's body language when I'm talking to them. _____

10. I'm perceived by my peers as confident when articulating my thoughts and opinions. _____

11. I can generally tell if someone is not interested in what I'm talking about. _____

12. I like socializing with my peers at a party. _____

13. I'm at ease when I'm with other students at school in a group discussion. _____

14. I'm comfortable asking my teachers questions and sharing my ideas in class. _____

15. Given the choice, I prefer to be with my friends rather than spending time alone. _____

16. Sometimes my friends perceive me as an expert when discussing a topic of interest to me. _____

17. I'm comfortable interacting with my peers in groups, teams, or in clubs at school or in the community. _____

18. I rarely have difficulty recounting my day with my family members when they ask. _____

19. I often ask questions and initiate conversations with my peers and family members. _____

20. I'm confident and sociable with people in almost any social setting. _____

Interpreting your questionnaire answers

Total your score. How many true answers did you have? How many false? Add the total for each. There are no wrong answers. Information from this exercise reveals your current level of self-awareness through identifying your own social perception. Collectively, answers may vary based on your age, developmental level, and social cognitive ability.

TRUE _____ I consider myself social.

FALSE _____ I do not consider myself social.

The information in this questionnaire answer key is only to be used as a student guide for improvement.

Project your thoughts, feelings, and ideas appropriately
Student–instructor feedback sheet: True or false questionnaire

Based on the results of your true or false questionnaire, discuss the following questions and answers with your instructor.

- How did you arrive at your answers in this exercise? Give some examples that support your answers.

_____

_____

_____

_____

- Does your instructor agree with your assessment of yourself? Why or why not?

_____

_____

_____

_____

- What did you learn most about yourself from this questionnaire?

_____

_____

_____

_____

- What answer(s) surprised you the most? Give examples.

_____

_____

_____

_____

- What answer(s) surprised you the least? Give examples.

_____

_____

_____

- What social skills would you like to improve upon? Be specific.

_____

_____

_____

- How will you accomplish this? Give an example.

_____

_____

_____

- What resources will you use or practice with? Give three examples.

_____

_____

_____

Topic planning MeNu principles

Starters

Starters are examples of how to start a "general" conversation with the person you're talking to. For example, when you want to engage socially with someone but don't know how to begin, choose from one of the following starter questions.

Note: "What?" and "How?" questions are great starters, as they are open-ended questions, prompting more than a yes or no answer from your conversational partner.

Starter examples

What are you up to today?

What's new with you lately?

What did you do over the weekend?

How did you do on the (insert subject) test?

What are your plans for (insert special event)?

What do you think about (insert any current event topic)?

What vacation do you have planned this (insert season)?

What are you doing for the (insert holiday)?

How is (insert pet name or friend name)?

What did you think of (insert movie or book title)?

After a starter question or two, move on to the main course topics.

Main course

The main course is the "meat and potatoes" of your conversation. You may find a topic of interest from your starter conversation that you'd like to expand on and continue to discuss as the main course topic. Otherwise, you can choose from one of the topics below to discuss with your conversational partner. Remember to engage in a dialogue, not a monologue. This means: ask questions and encourage input from your partner. Are you one to make statements and give opinions? If so, pay attention to your partner's face, gestures, and body language during your conversation. Have they commented as much as you have? Do they appear quiet and disinterested in your topic? Do they have questions, information, opinions?

Main course examples

SCHOOL

"I'm doing well in school this year. How about you? What's your best subject?"

"I can't believe I'm flunking geometry. Should I tell my parents?"

TEACHERS

"I really like my science teacher Ms. Smith. Who's your favorite teacher?"

"My history and English classes are really hard this year. Are any of your classes hard?"

FRIENDS

"Jack is my closest friend; I've known him since we started school. Who are some of your best friends?"

"I'm not that popular and don't have many friends. Do you have a lot of friends?"

HOBBIES

"I really like writing movie scripts. What do you like to do in your spare time?"

"My only hobby is surfing the internet. What are some of your hobbies?"

HOMEWORK

"My Spanish teacher gives a lot of homework. Which teacher gives you the most?"

"My teacher gives too much homework and I can't keep up. What should I do?"

SPORTS

"Our soccer team just won the championships. Do you play any sports?"

"I'm not very athletic and don't play sports. Do you play any?"

WEEKEND ACTIVITIES

"I'm going fishing with my dad this weekend. What are your weekend plans?"

"I don't have any plans for the weekend. Do you?"

CURRENT EVENTS/POLITICS

"I have a paper due in political science. Do you like politics?"

"There was a hurricane on the East Coast. Did you hear about it?"

SOCIAL EVENT

"I'd like to go to the Halloween dance, but I don't want to go alone. Who are you going with?"

"I don't like going to school dances. They're boring. What do you think?"

PROBLEMS/CONCERNS

"Our cat is sick and we might have to put him to sleep. Have you ever had to do that?"

"I think I sprained my ankle and baseball tryouts are today. What should I do?"

CLUBS

"I just joined a health club. Do you belong to any clubs?"

"My parents want me to join a club to meet other students, but I don't want to. What would you do if you were me?"

COMMUNITY ACTIVITIES

"I'm going to see the play *Oklahoma* tonight. Have you seen that play or any others?"

"I'm going to the Art Festival this weekend. Do you like art?"

HEALTH ISSUES

"I was just diagnosed with asthma. Do you have any health problems?"

"I was just given a new prescription for ADHD and it makes me feel different. What should I do?"

GOALS

"I'm planning to apply for college next Fall. What are you planning to do after high school?"

"I'm not sure what I want to do after I graduate high school. What are you thinking you'd like to do?"

FEELINGS

"Between schoolwork and my responsibilities at home, sometimes I feel overwhelmed. Do you ever feel that way? What do you do about it?"

"I feel depressed sometimes. What should I do when I feel that way?"

PARENTS/FAMILY

"My younger brother is very popular and always has friends over our house. Do you have any brothers?"

"I'm an only child. Do you have any siblings?"

Treats

Treats are generally statements that wrap up your conversation, indicating the end of your social exchange. Typically they are brief statements (not questions) that suggest your discussion is coming to a close.

Treat examples

"It was nice talking to you."

"I'll be in touch."

"Catch you later."

"I'm glad you could make it."

"It was nice to see you."

"I hope to see you again soon."

"It was nice meeting you."

"It was a pleasure to see you again."

"Thanks for the information."

"I appreciate your help."

"Have a good evening."

"Have a nice day."

"I enjoyed our time together—thanks."

"Take care."

"Be well."

"See you soon."

"Good luck."

"Goodbye."

"Thank you."

"Thanks, bye."

Practice using the social MeNu

Review the topic planning MeNu principles and create two social dialogues of your own. Incorporate a starter statement, a main course statement and/or question, and a treat closing statement. Students may use examples from pages 74–77.

Social dialogue: Family barbecue

Starter
(Start the conversation with a statement)

_____

_____

_____

Main course
(Convey the purpose of your conversation with a statement and/or question)

_____

_____

_____

_____

_____

Treat
(End the conversation with a statement)

_____

_____

_____

Social dialogue: Lunch break with a peer at school

Starter
(Start the conversation with a statement)

_____

_____

_____

Main course
(Convey the purpose of your conversation with a statement and/or question)

_____

_____

_____

_____

_____

Treat
(End the conversation with a statement)

_____

_____

_____

Personality test activity
Topic planning activity 1

The purpose of this exercise is to encourage students to think about themselves and others. The personality questionnaire is intended to elicit self-awareness, common interest, preferences, likes, dislikes, as well as topic implementation. Other questions in this activity describe scenarios whereby each student is asked to organize and prioritize their thoughts as if they were truly reacting to an unanticipated situation. The objective is to illustrate how casual conversations and recognizing commonalities (and differences) can create meaningful discussions. This process of social self-discovery can be used as a tool in future conversational topic planning.

The objective is to demonstrate the value of trading information and how it leads to topic planning for extended or future social exchanges. By completing this activity with another participant, each student will have ample information to initiate a conversation on a variety of topics.

Note: This personality test activity questionnaire is an interactive exercise. The same two participants must answer both sections of the questionnaire. The first two questionnaires are completed by you, the student: the first one about you and the second one about someone else. The third and fourth questionnaires are completed by someone else: one about themselves and the next about you. The objective is to have two people participate in both parts, compare their answers, and discuss the results with each other.

Personality test activity
Student "self" questionnaire: Participant #1

Your name: _____

Answer each question and explain your answer.

Example: What is your favorite book? *Gone with the Wind*, because it's a classic and I only read classics.

What is your favorite TV show? _____

_____

What is your favorite book? _____

_____

What is your favorite movie? _____

_____

Do you have a pet? If so, what's its name? _____

_____

What is your favorite thing to do on the weekend? _____

_____

Who is your best friend? _____

_____

Do you have a favorite sport? If so, what is it? _____

_____

What is your best subject in school? _____

_____

What is your favorite day of the week? _____

_____

What is your favorite hobby? _____

_____

What is your favorite food? _____

_____

Underline one answer and describe why it is your preference.

Example: Do you prefer reading or <u>math</u>? I prefer math because I understand math better than reading, and therefore I enjoy it more.

Do you prefer texting or talking? _____

_____

Do you prefer reading or math? _____

_____

Do you prefer writing or spelling? _____

_____

Do you prefer science, history, or politics?_____

_____

Do you prefer sailing or swimming? _____

_____

Do you prefer skiing or golfing? _____

_____

Do you prefer fact or fiction? _____

_____

Do you prefer cooking or eating? _____

_____

Do you prefer the beach or the mountains?_____

_____

Do you prefer sisters, brothers, both, or neither? _____

_____

Do you prefer board games or video games? _____

_____

Do you prefer inside or outside? _____

_____

Do you prefer people or pets? _____

_____

Do you prefer to be correct or to be happy? _____

_____

Do you prefer dogs, cats, or fish? _____

_____

Do you prefer friends or relatives? _____

_____

Do you prefer talking or listening? _____

_____

Do you prefer music or art? _____

_____

Do you prefer past, present, or future? _____

_____

Do you prefer *Star Wars* or *Star Trek*? _____

_____

Do you prefer sand or grass? _____

_____

Do you prefer sun or rain? _____

_____

Do you prefer flowers or trees? _____

_____

Do you prefer bugs or birds? _____

_____

Do you prefer football or baseball? _____

_____

Do you prefer dancing or jogging? _____

_____

Answer each question completely.

Example: If you could visit any place in the world, where would you visit and why? I would visit Italy because I love the culture, history, and food.

If you could visit any place in the world, where would you visit and why?

Answer: _____

_____

If you had only ten minutes to pack to go on a surprise vacation, what five things would you pack in your suitcase to take with you and why?

Answer:

1. _____

2. _____

3. _____

4. _____

5. _____

If you could do something incredible for a group of people, who would it be for and what would you do for them?

Answer: _____

_____

If you could do something nice for a complete stranger, what would it be and why?

Answer: _____

_____

What could you do to make the world a better place to live in?

Answer: _____

_____

Who knows you the best?

Answer: _____

_____

Personality test activity
Student topic planning questionnaire: Participant #1

Answer each question *about someone else* and explain your answer.

Who is this questionnaire about? _____
    (Example: friend, parent, teacher)

What is their favorite TV show? _____

_____

What is their favorite book? _____

_____

What is their favorite movie? _____

_____

Do they have a pet? If so, what's its name? _____

_____

What is their favorite thing to do at the weekend? _____

_____

Who is their best friend? _____

_____

Do they have a favorite sport? If so, what is it? _____

_____

What is their best subject in school? _____

_____

What is their favorite day of the week? _____

_____

What is their favorite hobby? _____

_____

What is their favorite food? _____

_____

Answer each question *about someone else*. Underline one answer and describe their preference and why.

Who is this questionnaire about? _____
   (Example: friend, parent, teacher)

Do they prefer texting or talking? _____

_____

Do they prefer reading or math? _____

_____

Do they prefer writing or spelling? _____

_____

Do they prefer science, history, or politics? _____

_____

Do they prefer sailing or swimming? _____

_____

Do they prefer skiing or golfing? _____

_____

Do they prefer fact or fiction? _____

_____

Do they prefer cooking or eating? _____

_____

Do they prefer the beach or the mountains? _____

_____

Do they prefer sisters, brothers, both, or neither? _____

_____

Do they prefer board games or video games? _____

_____

Do they prefer inside or outside? _____

_____

Do they prefer people or pets? _____

_____

Do they prefer to be correct or to be happy? _____

_____

Do they prefer dogs, cats, or fish? _____

_____

Do they prefer friends or relatives? _____

_____

Do they prefer talking or listening? _____

_____

Do they prefer music or art? _____

_____

Do they prefer past, present, or future? _____

_____

Do they prefer *Star Wars* or *Star Trek*? _____

_____

Do they prefer sand or grass? _____

_____

Do they prefer sun or rain? _____

_____

Do they prefer flowers or trees? _____

_____

Do they prefer bugs or birds? _____

_____

Do they prefer football or baseball? _____

_____

Do they prefer dancing or jogging? _____

_____

Answer each question *about someone else.*

Who is this questionnaire about? _____
  (Example: friend, parent, teacher)

If they could visit any place in the world, where would they visit and why?

Answer: _____

_____

If they had only ten minutes to pack to go on a surprise vacation, what five things would they pack in their suitcase to take with them and why?

Answer:

1. _____

2. _____

3. _____

4. _____

5. _____

If they could do something incredible for a group of people, who would it be for and what would they do for them?

Answer: _____

_____

If they could do something nice for a complete stranger, what would it be and why?

Answer: _____

_____

What could they do to make the world a better place to live in?

Answer: _____

_____

Who knows them the best?

Answer: _____

_____

Personality test activity
Student "self" questionnaire: Participant #2

This section is to be completed by another student or "participant #2" so that "participant #1" can compare their answers to participant #2. Answer each question and explain your answer.

Participant #2

Your name: _____

Example: What is your favorite book? *Gone with the Wind*, because it's a classic and I only read classics.

What is your favorite TV show? _____

_____

What is your favorite book? _____

_____

What is your favorite movie? _____

_____

Do you have a pet? If so, what's its name? _____

_____

What is your favorite thing to do at the weekend? _____

_____

Who is your best friend? _____

_____

Do you have a favorite sport? If so, what is it? _____

_____

What is your best subject in school? _____

_____

What is your favorite day of the week? _____

_____

What is your favorite hobby? _____

_____

What is your favorite food? _____

_____

Underline one answer and describe why it is your preference.

Example: Do you prefer reading or <u>math</u>? I prefer math because I understand math better than reading, and therefore I enjoy it more.

Do you prefer texting or talking? _____

_____

Do you prefer reading or math? _____

_____

Do you prefer writing or spelling? _____

_____

Do you prefer science, history or politics? _____

_____

Do you prefer sailing or swimming? _____

_____

Do you prefer skiing or golfing? _____

_____

Do you prefer fact or fiction? _____

_____

Do you prefer cooking or eating? _____

_____

Do you prefer the beach or the mountains? _____

_____

Do you prefer sisters, brothers, both, or neither? _____

_____

Do you prefer board games or video games? _____

_____

Do you prefer inside or outside? _____

_____

Do you prefer people or pets? _____

_____

Do you prefer to be correct or to be happy? _____

_____

Do you prefer dogs, cats, or fish? _____

_____

Do you prefer friends or relatives? _____

_____

Do you prefer talking or listening? _____

_____

Do you prefer music or art? _____

_____

Do you prefer past, present, or future? _____

_____

Do you prefer *Star Wars* or *Star Trek*? _____

_____

Do you prefer sand or grass? _____

_____

Do you prefer sun or rain? _____

_____

Do you prefer flowers or trees? _____

_____

Do you prefer bugs or birds? _____

_____

Do you prefer football or baseball? _____

_____

Do you prefer dancing or jogging? _____

_____

Answer each question completely.

Example: If you could visit any place in the world, where would you visit and why? I would visit Italy because I love the culture, history, and food.

If you could visit any place in the world, where would you visit and why?

Answer: _____

_____

If you had only ten minutes to pack to go on a surprise vacation, what five things would you pack in your suitcase to take with you?

Answer:

1. _____

2. _____

3. _____

4. _____

5. _____

If you could do something incredible for a group of people, who would it be for and what would you do for them?

Answer: _____

_____

If you could do something nice for a complete stranger, what would it be and why?

Answer: _____

_____

What could you do to make the world a better place to live in?

Answer: _____

_____

Who knows you the best?

Answer: _____

_____

Personality test activity
Student topic planning questionnaire: Participant #2

Answer each question *about someone else* and explain your answer.

Who is this questionnaire about? _____
   (Example: friend, parent, teacher)

What is their favorite TV show? _____

_____

What is their favorite book? _____

_____

What is their favorite movie? _____

_____

Do they have a pet? If so, what's its name? _____

_____

What is their favorite thing to do at the weekend? _____

_____

Who is their best friend? _____

_____

Do they have a favorite sport? If so, what is it? _____

_____

What is their best subject in school? _____

_____

What is their favorite day of the week? _____

_____

What is their favorite hobby? _____

_____

What is their favorite food? _____

_____

Answer each question *about someone else*. Underline one answer and describe their preference and why.

Who is this questionnaire about? _____
   (Example: friend, parent, teacher)

Do they prefer texting or talking? _____
_____

Do they prefer reading or math? _____
_____

Do they prefer writing or spelling? _____
_____

Do they prefer science, history, or politics? _____
_____

Do they prefer sailing or swimming? _____
_____

Do they prefer skiing or golfing? _____
_____

Do they prefer fact or fiction? _____
_____

Do they prefer cooking or eating? _____
_____

Do they prefer the beach or the mountains? _____
_____

Do they prefer sisters, brothers, both, or neither? _____
_____

Do they prefer board games or video games? _____
_____

Do they prefer inside or outside? _____
_____

Do they prefer people or pets? _____

_____

Do they prefer to be correct or to be happy? _____

_____

Do they prefer dogs, cats, or fish? _____

_____

Do they prefer friends or relatives? _____

_____

Do they prefer talking or listening? _____

_____

Do they prefer music or art? _____

_____

Do they prefer past, present, or future? _____

_____

Do they prefer *Star Wars* or *Star Trek*? _____

_____

Do they prefer sand or grass? _____

_____

Do they prefer sun or rain? _____

_____

Do they prefer flowers or trees? _____

_____

Do they prefer bugs or birds? _____

_____

Do they prefer football or baseball? _____

_____

Do they prefer dancing or jogging? _____

_____

Answer each question *about someone else.*

Who is this questionnaire about? _____

    (Example: friend, parent, teacher)

If they could visit any place in the world, where would they visit and why?

Answer: _____

_____

If they had only ten minutes to pack to go on a surprise vacation, what five things would they pack in their suitcase to take with them?

    Answer:

1. _____

2. _____

3. _____

4. _____

5. _____

If they could do something incredible for a group of people, who would it be for and what would they do for them?

Answer: _____

_____

If they could do something nice for a complete stranger, what would it be and why?

Answer: _____

_____

What could they do to make the world a better place to live in?

Answer: _____

_____

Who knows them the best?

Answer: _____

_____

Personality test activity
Discussion questions

Share your answers with your questionnaire partner. Compare your answers with theirs and answer the following questions:

- Did you discover anything new about yourself from this exercise?

_____

_____

_____

- Did any of your answers surprise you?

_____

_____

_____

- Was this exercise challenging for you?

_____

_____

_____

- Did you find this exercise useful?

_____

_____

_____

- What information was interesting to you?

_____

_____

_____

- Do you feel more prepared to start a topic of conversation following the information gained from this exercise?

_____

_____

_____

- Who was your questionnaire partner? _____

- Did you learn anything new about your questionnaire partner?

_____

_____

- Were you accurate in your answers describing your questionnaire partner?

_____

_____

- Was your questionnaire partner accurate in describing you?

_____

_____

- What information can you use from this questionnaire to engage in a future conversation?

_____

_____

_____

Using the MeNu as a template, and based on the information you have obtained from this exercise, practice starting, maintaining, and ending a shared conversation using the following MeNu templates.

Personality test activity
Practice using social MeNu templates 1

Using information from the personality test activity, create a dialogue between you and your questionnaire partner.

Topic

(Example: favorite book, movie, sport, hobby, or subject in school)

_____

_____

Starter

(Start a conversation with an introduction statement)

_____

_____

Main course

(Convey the purpose of your conversation with a statement and/or question)

_____

_____

_____

_____

Treat

(End the conversation with a statement)

_____

_____

Personality test activity
Practice using social MeNu templates 2

Using information from the personality test activity, create a dialogue between you and your questionnaire partner.

Topic

(Example: favorite place to visit, food, music, or art)

_____

_____

Starter

(Start a conversation with an introduction statement)

_____

_____

Main course

(Convey the purpose of your conversation with a statement and/or question)

_____

_____

_____

_____

Treat

(End the conversation with a statement)

_____

_____

Personality test activity
Practice using social MeNu templates 3

Using information from the personality test activity, create a dialogue between you and your questionnaire partner.

Topic

(Example: compare answers to "If you could do something incredible for a group of people, who would it be for and what would you do for them?")

_____

_____

Starter

(Start a conversation with an introduction statement)

_____

_____

Main course

(Convey the purpose of your conversation with a statement and/or question)

_____

_____

_____

_____

Treat

(End the conversation with a statement)

_____

_____

Social situation activity
Topic planning activity 2

On the following blank templates create a fictional social dialogue for each of the five topics. Below is a worked example for the first social scenario.

1. Your friend lost his wallet and can't buy his bus ticket to get home from school. What do you say to him?

2. You are pet-sitting your neighbor's bird and now the bird is sick. What do you say to your neighbor?

3. You borrowed your friend's bike and now it has a flat tire. What do you say to your friend?

4. You misplaced your dad's car keys and he's late for an important appointment. What do you say to your dad?

5. Your brother borrowed your shin pads without asking and now you can't find them for your big game. What do you say to your brother?

Example 1
Food for thought

Think of the MeNu as a social reference on how to:

Starter

Start a conversation with an introduction statement
    Friend: "I have a problem."
    You: "What's the problem?"

Main course

Convey the purpose of your conversation with a statement and/or question
    Friend: "I just realized I've lost my wallet and need bus fare to get home. Can I borrow $5 from you? I promise to pay you back tomorrow?"
    You: "Sure."

Treat

End the conversation with a statement
    Friend: "Thank you for helping me out."
    You: "You are welcome."

Social situation activity
MeNu template

Social scenario

Your friend lost his wallet and can't buy his bus ticket to get home from school. What do you say to him? Describe the social interaction.

Starter

(Start a conversation with an introduction statement)

_____

_____

_____

Main course

(Convey the purpose of your conversation with a statement and/or question)

_____

_____

_____

_____

_____

Treat

(End the conversation with a statement)

_____

_____

_____

Social situation activity
MeNu template

Social scenario

You are pet-sitting your neighbor's bird and now the bird is sick. What do you say to your neighbor? Describe the social interaction.

Starter

(Start a conversation with an introduction statement)

_____

_____

_____

Main course

(Convey the purpose of your conversation with a statement and/or question)

_____

_____

_____

_____

_____

Treat

(End the conversation with a statement)

_____

_____

_____

Social situation activity
MeNu template

Social scenario

You borrowed your friend's bike and now it has a flat tire. What do you say to your friend? Describe the social interaction.

Starter

(Start a conversation with an introduction statement)

_____

_____

_____

Main course

(Convey the purpose of your conversation with a statement and/or question)

_____

_____

_____

_____

_____

Treat

(End the conversation with a statement)

_____

_____

_____

Social situation activity
MeNu template

Social scenario

You misplaced your dad's car keys and he's late for an important appointment. What do you say to your dad? Describe the social interaction.

Starter

(Start a conversation with an introduction statement)

_____

_____

_____

Main course

(Convey the purpose of your conversation with a statement and/or question)

_____

_____

_____

_____

_____

Treat

(End the conversation with a statement)

_____

_____

_____

Social situation activity
MeNu template

Social scenario

Your brother borrowed your shin pads without asking and now you can't find them for your big game. What do you say to your brother? Describe the social interaction.

Starter

(Start a conversation with an introduction statement)

_____

_____

_____

Main course

(Convey the purpose of your conversation with a statement and/or question)

_____

_____

_____

_____

_____

Treat

(End the conversation with a statement)

_____

_____

_____

Social situation activity
Discussion questions

Review the MeNu template with your instructor and answer and discuss the following questions:

- When creating the fictional social dialogues in the last activity, which scenario was most challenging? Why? What could you do differently next time?

_____

_____

_____

_____

- Which social scenario was the least challenging to address? Why?

_____

_____

_____

_____

- Did you have difficulty initiating a dialogue when there was a social conflict? In what way? What could you do differently?

_____

_____

_____

_____

- How would you handle a similar social situation in the future? Describe and explain the social situation.

_____

_____

_____

_____

Social situations
Topic planning activity 3

Using the MeNu template as reference, create a fictional social dialogue for each of the following topics, then role play each social scenario with another person.

Dialogue 1

Special event situation

You and your best friend have tickets to the last show of the traveling circus. Your friend lost her ticket and can't afford to buy another one. You still want to go even if she can't. What do you say to your friend?

Starter

(Start a conversation with an introduction statement)

_____

_____

Main course

(Convey the purpose of your conversation with a statement and/or question)

_____

_____

_____

_____

Treat

(End the conversation with a statement)

_____

_____

Social situations
Topic planning activity 3

Using the MeNu template as reference, create a fictional social dialogue for each of the following topics, then role play each social scenario with another person.

Dialogue 2

Team sport situation

Your team made the final playoffs in basketball. Your coach intends to play the key players which may not include you. Although this is a critical game, you want to have equal play time. What do say to the coach or team members?

Starter

(Start a conversation with an introduction statement)

_____

_____

Main course

(Convey the purpose of your conversation with a statement and/or question)

_____

_____

_____

_____

Treat

(End the conversation with a statement)

_____

_____

Social situations
Topic planning activity 3

Using the MeNu template as reference, create a fictional social dialogue for each of the following topics, then role play each social scenario with another person.

Dialogue 3

Social special event

You and your family are invited to your cousin's wedding. It's a formal event and your mother wants you to wear your older brother's suit. You have a tactile aversion to most fabrics and you know you'll be uncomfortable wearing the suit. What do you say to your mother?

Starter

(Start a conversation with an introduction statement)

_____

_____

Main course

(Convey the purpose of your conversation with a statement and/or question)

_____

_____

_____

_____

Treat

(End the conversation with a statement)

_____

_____

Social situations
Topic planning activity 3

Using the MeNu template as reference, create a fictional social dialogue for each of the following topics, then role play each social scenario with another person.

Dialogue 4

Social anxiety situation

Your parents plan to send you and your brother to a sleep away camp for two weeks in the summer. Although you like "day camps," you are anxious about attending sleep away camp for the first time with people you don't know. What do you do or say to your parents?

Starter

(Start a conversation with an introduction statement)

_____

_____

Main course

(Convey the purpose of your conversation with a statement and/or question)

_____

_____

_____

_____

Treat

(End the conversation with a statement)

_____

_____

Social situations
Topic planning activity 3

Using the MeNu template as reference, create a fictional social dialogue for each of the following topics, then role play each social scenario with another person.

Dialogue 5

Social conflict situation

You and your neighbor are playing softball in the street near your house when you hit the ball and accidentally break a car window. The car alarm goes off and you can't handle the loud noise. What do you do? What do you say?

Starter

(Start a conversation with an introduction statement)

_____

_____

Main course

(Convey the purpose of your conversation with a statement and/or question)

_____

_____

_____

_____

Treat

(End the conversation with a statement)

_____

_____

Social situations
Topic planning activity 3

Using the MeNu template as reference, create a fictional social dialogue for each of the following topics, then role play each social scenario with another person.

Dialogue 6

Social volunteer situation

Your favorite teacher asks you to volunteer after school to help tutor another student in science lab. You're good in science and want to do it, but you promised your parents you'd watch your little sister after school that day. What do you say to your teacher and/or parents?

Starter

(Start a conversation with an introduction statement)

_____

_____

Main course

(Convey the purpose of your conversation with a statement and/or question)

_____

_____

_____

_____

Treat

(End the conversation with a statement)

_____

_____

Social situations
Dialogue feedback sheet

Explain and describe the interaction in each social dialogue with your instructor.

Dialogue 1

Special event situation

Was this social situation difficult to address? _____

Why or why not? _____

_____

_____

_____

Dialogue 2

Team sport situation

Was this social situation difficult to address? _____

Why or why not? _____

_____

_____

_____

Dialogue 3

Social special event

Was this social situation difficult to address? _____

Why or why not? _____

_____

_____

_____

Dialogue 4

Social anxiety situation

Was this social situation difficult to address? _____

Why or why not? _____

_____

_____

_____

Dialogue 5

Social conflict situation

Was this social situation difficult to address? _____

Why or why not? _____

_____

_____

_____

Dialogue 6

Social volunteer situation

Was this situation difficult to address? _____

Why or why not? _____

_____

_____

_____

Difficult social situations
Topic planning activity 4

Topic planning is often difficult when you are faced with uncomfortable social situations that are difficult to address, such as tolerating an awkward social situation among your peer group, negotiating a compromise with a classmate, or feeling betrayed by a friend. Answer each social scenario question below and describe your response.

Use the MeNu templates on the following pages to create a social dialogue for each of the three social scenarios below. Review and discuss each of your answers with your instructor.

- What do you say when you are having trouble tolerating an awkward social situation among your peer group?

  Example: Several of your peers are discussing the details of a party they had gone to over the weekend, knowing you were not there because you had not been invited.

- What do you say when you're negotiating a compromise with a classmate?

  Example: You and a classmate are collaborating together on a school project and can't agree on how the project information should be presented.

- What do you say when you feel betrayed by a friend?

  Example: You recently broke up with your boyfriend and discover your best friend is dating him.

Difficult social situations
MeNu template

What do you say when you are having trouble tolerating an awkward social situation among your peer group?

Scenario

(Create the scenario between you and a peer)

_____

_____

Starter

(Start a conversation with an introduction statement)

_____

_____

Main course

(Convey the purpose of your conversation with a statement and/or question)

_____

_____

_____

_____

Treat

(End the conversation with a statement)

_____

_____

Difficult social situations
MeNu template

What do you say when you're negotiating a compromise with a classmate?

Scenario

(Create the scenario between you and classmate)

_____

_____

Starter

(Start a conversation with an introduction statement)

_____

_____

Main course

(Convey the purpose of your conversation with a statement and/or question)

_____

_____

_____

_____

Treat

(End the conversation with a statement)

_____

_____

Difficult social situations
MeNu template

What do you say when you feel betrayed by a friend?

Scenario

(Create the scenario between you and a friend)

_____

_____

Starter

(Start a conversation with an introduction statement)

_____

_____

Main course

(Convey the purpose of your conversation with a statement and/or question)

_____

_____

_____

_____

Treat

(End the conversation with a statement)

_____

_____

Topic planning discussion questions

Review each questionnaire answer with your instructor. Record and discuss each social scenario and your answers.

- What topic planning techniques were easiest for you to identify with?

_____

_____

_____

_____

- Describe a social scenario that was most difficult for you to plan a topic around?

_____

_____

_____

_____

- What did you learn about yourself regarding how to maintain a conversation from this exercise?

_____

_____

_____

_____

- In this exercise, what was the most socially challenging situation?

_____

_____

_____

_____

- Were specific topics more interesting to explore than others? If so which ones?

_____

_____

_____

_____

- What information or techniques in this section will you use to assist you in future social conversations and/or situations? Why?

_____

_____

_____

_____

Chapter 2 summary

In this chapter, students answered questionnaires regarding perspective-taking scenarios. They interpreted, discussed, and recorded their thoughts, feelings, and ideas about their experiences with an instructor. In the second part of the chapter, students developed topic-planning strategies using interactive activities and social MeNu principles as a social guide.

Goal

Students examined how to project their thoughts, feelings, and ideas appropriately while identifying the perspectives of others in various social interactions.

Objective

Using topic examples from the Starter MeNu, students understood the concept of topic planning. Students implemented their ideas and interests as these related to a topic of conversation in the prescribed discussion questions outlined in this chapter.

MeNu Practicing Topics

Practice your social exchanges with others frequently

In this chapter: The practice of communicating socially

- Practice your social exchanges with others frequently
  - Social scenario questionnaire 3: Effective social communication
  - Student–instructor feedback sheet: Social scenario questionnaire 3
  - Discussion questions: Social scenario questionnaire 3
  - Social scenario summaries 1–15
  - Student-generated social scenarios 1–3
- Social scenario discussion questions
- Chapter 3 summary

Goal

In this chapter students will practice sharing ideas, thoughts, and interests socially as they interact with each other in chapter exercises.

Objective

Students and instructors will role-play social exchanges in prescribed social settings, using the MeNu worksheets for referencing.

Four core concepts to improve social communication:

- **prepare** to communicate socially
- **project** your thoughts, feelings, and ideas appropriately
- **practice** your social exchanges with others frequently
- **produce** an effective level of communication.

Practice your social exchanges with others frequently

Social scenario questionnaire 3: Effective social communication

There are ten questions in this section. Select answers that best describe how you think you would react in the social scenarios below. You may select "other" to create your own answer.

1. An acquaintance calls you and invites you to see a movie at the local theater in town. You don't care for the movie they have suggested. You:

    a. suggest a different movie

    b. decline their offer, but suggest a different type of outing

    c. avoid the potential conflict and tell them you're busy and can't go

    d. annoyed, tell them that you don't like the movie they've selected and refuse to go

    e. other: _____

2. You want to attend the school dance, but you don't want to go with the friend that has invited you. You:

    a. politely decline and ask a different friend if they'd like to meet you there

    b. attend the dance and try to enjoy yourself despite your discomfort

    c. avoid the issue altogether by staying home instead

    d. get upset and vow never to attend any more social events

    e. other: _____

3. You've been waiting patiently in line at the grocery store when someone cuts right in front of you at the check-out. You:

    a. assume it was not intentional and politely tell the person that you were next in line

    b. say nothing even if you are annoyed

    c. rudely tell the person you are next in line, not them

    d. are angry and decide to leave the store abruptly

    e. other: _____

4. You're playing a card game with some friends and notice that one of them is cheating. You:

    a. say nothing, but decide to exclude the cheater from all future games

    b. continue playing, but announce to everyone that there is a cheater among you without revealing their identity to the group

    c. expose the cheater to the group and request that they immediately stop cheating or stop playing the game

    d. get extremely upset and refuse to finish the game

    e. other: _____

5. You're involved in a group presentation at school with four other students. Your group can't agree on a topic and thus can't complete the presentation. Your assignment is due the following day. You:

    a. appoint yourself leader of the group and convince your group to work as a team

    b. explain the time limit on the presentation and try to negotiate a topic quickly with the other students

    c. refuse to work with a group that can't agree and ask to be put into another group immediately

    d. realize this could affect your grade and call in sick the day your presentation is due

    e. other: _____

6. You and a classmate are studying for a science test. You know the material quite well whereas your classmate seems to be struggling. On the day of the exam you notice that your classmate appears to be cheating on the test. You:

    a. tell your classmate you saw them cheating and offer to study with them for the next test so they won't need to cheat

    b. assume science isn't their best subject and pretend not to have noticed

    c. turn them in to the teacher

    d. decide you can no longer associate with them because of their behavior

    e. other: _____

7. You are at a retail store and notice a customer stealing an item from the store. You:

    a. immediately tell a store clerk what you saw

    b. decide it doesn't involve you and walk away from the incident

    c. tell your parents what you saw later that night

    d. abruptly grab the customer's hand to stop them from stealing the item

    e. other: _____

8. You're at the bus stop waiting for the school bus when a stranger approaches you and asks you for money. You:

    a. don't respond, walk away and ignore them

    b. briefly tell them that you have no money to give them and walk away

    c. assume they must need it if they asked you, and give them all the money in your wallet

    d. explain to them they should seek employment if they need money

    e. other: _____

9. You're almost out of your prescription medication and need to pick up a refill at the pharmacy. When you arrive, you realize that you don't have enough money with you to purchase your refill prescription. You:

    a. calmly ask the pharmacist to hold on to your prescription and you'll pick it up soon

    b. tell the pharmacist to hold on to it while you immediately go home to get the money and quickly return to pay for it

    c. tell the pharmacist you are a good customer and ask them to give you the refill prescription anyway, and that you'll pay them sometime soon

    d. panic and have a meltdown in the drug store

e. other: _____

_____

10. You attempt to return a book you'd received as a gift to your local book store. The book store cashier quickly informs you that you cannot return any book without a receipt. You:

  a. ask the cashier if you can exchange the book for store credit instead

  b. understand their return policy and return home, disappointed with your book

  c. are upset and try to convince the cashier to accept the book without a receipt anyway

  d. think their return policy is ridiculous and ask to speak to the manager in an effort to get your way

  e. other: _____

_____

Interpreting your questionnaire answers

Total your score. How many a, b, c, d, or e answers did you have? Add the total for each. There are no wrong answers. Information from this exercise reveals your current level of effective social communication. Collectively, answers may vary based on your age, developmental level, and social cognitive ability.

a_____ proficient

b_____ requires practice

c   _____ needs assistance

d_____ challenged

e_____ other

The information in this questionnaire answer key is only to be used as a student guide.

Practice your social exchanges with others frequently
Student–instructor feedback sheet: Social scenario questionnaire 3

Questionnaire feedback worksheets are used as a method to discuss further each questionnaire answer with your instructor. Explain your observations of the social communication in each scenario.

Were these social situations difficult for you to address?
Why or why not? Explain.

1. An acquaintance calls you and invites you to see a movie at the local theater in town. You don't care for the movie they have suggested. You: _____

    _____

    _____

2. You want to attend the school dance, but you don't want to go with the friend that has invited you. You: _____

    _____

    _____

3. You've been waiting patiently in line at the grocery store when someone cuts right in front of you at the check-out. You: _____

    _____

    _____

4. You're playing a card game with some friends and notice that one of them is cheating. You: _____

    _____

    _____

5. You're involved in a group presentation at school with four other students. Your group can't agree on a topic and thus can't complete the presentation. Your assignment is due the following day. You: _____

    _____

    _____

6. You and a classmate are studying for a science test. You know the material quite well, whereas your classmate seems to be struggling. On the day of the exam, you notice that your classmate appears to be cheating on the test. You:_____

_____

_____

7. You are at a retail store and notice a customer stealing an item from the store. You: _____

_____

_____

8. You're at the bus stop waiting for the bus to take you to school, when a stranger approaches you and asks you for money. You: _____

_____

_____

9. You're almost out of your prescription medication and need to pick up a refill at the pharmacy. When you arrive, you realize that you don't have enough money with you to purchase your refill prescription. You: _____

_____

_____

10. You attempt to return a book you'd received as a gift to your local book store. The book store cashier quickly informs you that you cannot return any book without a receipt. You:_____

_____

_____

Practice your social exchanges with others frequently
Discussion questions: Social scenario questionnaire 3

Review each questionnaire answer with your instructor and answer and discuss the following questions:

- Could you relate to any of the social scenarios in this section? If so which ones?

_____

_____

_____

_____

- Can you describe similar social experiences and or reactions? Explain.

_____

_____

_____

_____

- Did you discover anything surprising about yourself from this exercise?

_____

_____

_____

_____

- Which social questions in this section could you not identify with at all?

_____

_____

_____

_____

- What particular areas of social communication are most challenging for you currently?

  _____

  _____

  _____

  _____

- What do you typically do in similar socially uncomfortable situations? Give an example.

  _____

  _____

  _____

  _____

- Did you find this exercise helpful? Why or why not?

  _____

  _____

  _____

  _____

- Describe yourself in a successful social situation. Give an example.

  _____

  _____

  _____

  _____

- What did you learn from this section that you will apply to future social exchanges?

  _____

  _____

  _____

  _____

Practice your social exchanges with others frequently
Social scenario summaries

Effective social communication requires practice. Practicing a response to an unanticipated social situation helps to generalize an effective social reaction. Using MeNu templates, create a social dialogue including a starter statement, main course statement/question, and treat statement for each of the 15 social scenario summaries. Then practice your social dialogue by "role playing" each social scenario with another person.

Social scenario 1

You've asked a schoolmate out on a date and they've happily accepted. Right before you are supposed to meet them, they text you claiming they are sick and need to cancel. The next day, you find out that they weren't sick at all and had actually gone to a party with another friend. You can't believe that you've been lied to. How does this make you feel? How do you handle the social situation effectively? Do you confront your schoolmate? Explain.

MeNu template

Starter

(Start a conversation with an introduction statement)

_____

_____

_____

Main course

(Convey the purpose of your conversation with a statement and/or question)

_____

_____

_____

_____

_____

Treat

(End the conversation with a statement)

_____

_____

_____

Social scenario 2

You are enjoying dinner with a friend at your favorite Italian restaurant when you become distracted by a couple arguing at a nearby table. Although you are able to ignore the argument, your friend cannot and becomes verbally involved in their situation. The situation escalates, voices are raised, and you can't believe this is happening right in front of you. How does this make you feel? How do you handle the social situation effectively? Do you confront your friend about their actions? Explain.

MeNu template

Starter

(Start a conversation with an introduction statement)

_____

_____

_____

Main course

(Convey the purpose of your conversation with a statement and/or question)

_____

_____

_____

_____

_____

Treat

(End the conversation with a statement)

_____

_____

_____

Social scenario 3

You tell your best friend that you are applying for a summer job at the comic book store in town to earn money for an upcoming school trip. You inform your friend that there is only one position available and you intend to get it. When you arrive at your scheduled job interview that afternoon, you see your friend sitting in the waiting room applying for the exact same job. How does this make you feel? How do you handle the social situation effectively? Do you confront your friend about their intentions? Explain.

MeNu template

Starter

(Start a conversation with an introduction statement)

_____

_____

_____

Main course

(Convey the purpose of your conversation with a statement and/or question)

_____

_____

_____

_____

_____

Treat

(End the conversation with a statement)

_____

_____

_____

Social scenario 4

You find out that your father has been offered a promotion at work and will need to travel out of town most weekends for an extended period of time. For years you've spent every Friday night with your father having dinner and seeing the latest movie. You suddenly realize that your special time with him can no longer take place on Fridays because of the travel required for his new job. How do you feel about this new situation? How will you handle this new information and react to it effectively? Will you discuss your feelings with your father or anyone else? Explain.

MeNu template

Starter

(Start a conversation with an introduction statement)

_____

_____

_____

Main course

(Convey the purpose of your conversation with a statement and/or question)

_____

_____

_____

_____

_____

Treat

(End the conversation with a statement)

_____

_____

_____

Social scenario 5

You and your younger brother both try out for your high school track team. You've wanted to join the track team for years and after lots of practice you've finally gotten up the courage to try out. Shortly after the selection process began, you find out that your brother made the team and you did not. Your brother is ecstatic, while you are terribly disappointed. How do you feel about this news? How will you handle this new information effectively? Will you discuss your feelings with your brother? Explain.

MeNu template

Starter

(Start a conversation with an introduction statement)

_____

_____

_____

Main course

(Convey the purpose of your conversation with a statement and/or question)

_____

_____

_____

_____

_____

Treat

(End the conversation with a statement)

_____

_____

_____

Social scenario 6

You are in your final year of high school and your parents are away for the night. They specifically tell you to stay home with your seven-year-old sister that evening to watch over her. The same night you are invited to go to a Yu-Gi-Oh tournament with friends from school. You really want to go! After explaining the circumstances to your sister, she insists that she doesn't mind staying home alone. What will you do? How will you handle this social situation effectively? What are your concerns? Will you discuss your decision with anyone? Explain.

McNu template

Starter

(Start a conversation with an introduction statement)

_____

_____

_____

Main course

(Convey the purpose of your conversation with a statement and/or question)

_____

_____

_____

_____

_____

Treat

(End the conversation with a statement)

_____

_____

_____

Social scenario 7

You're celebrating graduation night at a beach party with a group of friends. You and your friends are laughing, telling stories, and sitting by a bonfire when you notice several of your friends drinking alcohol and passing it around. Although you don't drink alcohol, you want to stay and be part of the "in crowd." How do you feel about this situation? Are you uncomfortable? How will you handle this social situation effectively? Will you share your feelings with any of your friends at the beach party or parents? Explain.

MeNu template

Starter

(Start a conversation with an introduction statement)

_____

_____

_____

Main course

(Convey the purpose of your conversation with a statement and/or question)

_____

_____

_____

_____

_____

Treat

(End the conversation with a statement)

_____

_____

_____

Social scenario 8

You and your 17-year-old cousin are downtown and your cousin wants to get a tattoo/piercing. You know his parents (your aunt and uncle) would be upset if they knew, so you promise your cousin you won't tell them anything. Later, your mother figures it out and wants you to tell your aunt and uncle about your cousin's tattoo/ piercing. How do you feel about this social situation? How will you handle this social situation effectively? Will you tell your aunt and uncle or honor your promise to your cousin? Explain.

MeNu template

Starter

(Start a conversation with an introduction statement)

_____

_____

_____

Main course

(Convey the purpose of your conversation with a statement and/or question)

_____

_____

_____

_____

_____

Treat

(End the conversation with a statement)

_____

_____

_____

Social scenario 9

You won two tickets to a sold-out concert by your favorite rock band. Two of your buddies like the same band and both really want to go with you to the concert. You are good friends with each of them and don't know who to invite to the concert. How will you decide who to give the extra concert ticket to? How will you handle this social situation effectively? Is the decision difficult for you? Will you feel awkward? Explain.

MeNu template

Starter

(Start a conversation with an introduction statement)

_____

_____

_____

Main course

(Convey the purpose of your conversation with a statement and/or question)

_____

_____

_____

_____

_____

Treat

(End the conversation with a statement)

_____

_____

_____

Social scenario 10

You think birthdays are special and you've made it a point to memorize and acknowledge everyone's birthday in your classes at school. Unfortunately, when your birthday arrives, you can't believe that none of your friends remembered. You feel badly and want to be acknowledged on your special day, but you feel silly reminding your friends. What will you do? How will you handle this social situation effectively? How will you make yourself feel better? Explain.

MeNu template

Starter

(Start a conversation with an introduction statement)

_____

_____

_____

Main course

(Convey the purpose of your conversation with a statement and/or question)

_____

_____

_____

_____

_____

Treat

(End the conversation with a statement)

_____

_____

_____

Social scenario 11

You've had a major crush on a classmate for months and you've finally gotten up the courage to ask them to a school football game. Unfortunately, they turn down your invitation, but tell you they are flattered by your invitation. What do you do? How does that make you feel? Will you ever ask them out again? What can be inferred? How will you handle this social situation effectively? Explain.

MeNu template

Starter

(Start a conversation with an introduction statement)

_____

_____

_____

Main course

(Convey the purpose of your conversation with a statement and/or question)

_____

_____

_____

_____

_____

Treat

(End the conversation with a statement)

_____

_____

_____

Social scenario 12

You heard a classmate bragging about hacking into another classmate's computer and infecting it with a computer virus. Although you don't want to get involved, you feel that it is your moral obligation to tell someone what you've heard. Whom will you tell? What will you do? How will you handle this social situation effectively? Explain.

MeNu template

Starter

(Start a conversation with an introduction statement)

_____

_____

_____

Main course

(Convey the purpose of your conversation with a statement and/or question)

_____

_____

_____

_____

_____

Treat

(End the conversation with a statement)

_____

_____

_____

Social scenario 13

There's a new student at your school. And although you've noticed they're spending every lunch period by themselves and you'd like to befriend them, you are terribly shy yourself and uncomfortable initiating social interactions. What will you do? How will you address this social situation effectively? Explain.

MeNu template

Starter

(Start a conversation with an introduction statement)

_____

_____

_____

Main course

(Convey the purpose of your conversation with a statement and/or question)

_____

_____

_____

_____

_____

Treat

(End the conversation with a statement)

_____

_____

_____

Social scenario 14

The mall is closing and you and a friend become separated while shopping. You are supposed to get a ride home from your friend, but you don't have your cell phone with you and can't call them. What will you do? How will you handle this social situation effectively? What do you think your friend is thinking? How will you make yourself feel better? Explain.

MeNu template

Starter

(Start a conversation with an introduction statement)

_____

_____

_____

Main course
(Convey the purpose of your conversation with a statement and/or question)

_____
_____
_____
_____
_____

Treat
(End the conversation with a statement)

_____
_____
_____

Social scenario 15

When you arrive home late one cold, rainy night, you notice the gate to your yard had been left open. When you call your dog's name and he doesn't come, you realize that he's missing. That's when your sister admits that she'd accidentally left the back gate open that morning. What will you do? How will you handle this social situation effectively? What do you say to your sister? Are you upset? How will you make yourself feel better? Explain.

MeNu template

Starter
(Start a conversation with an introduction statement)

_____
_____
_____

Main course

(Convey the purpose of your conversation with a statement and/or question)

_____

_____

_____

_____

_____

Treat

(End the conversation with a statement)

_____

_____

_____

Practice your social exchanges with others frequently
Student-generated social scenario 1

MeNu template

Social scenario

(Create a social scenario about a conflict between you and a friend or classmate)

_____

_____

_____

Starter

(Start a conversation with an introduction statement)

_____

_____

_____

Main course

(Convey the purpose of your conversation with a statement and/or question)

_____

_____

_____

_____

_____

Treat

(End the conversation with a statement)

_____

_____

_____

Practice your social exchanges with others frequently
Student-generated social scenario 2

MeNu template

Social scenario

(Create a social scenario about how you felt when your driving instructor told you that you did not pass your driver's exam to get your driver's permit.)

Starter

(Start a conversation with an introduction statement)

_____

_____

_____

Main course

(Convey the purpose of your conversation with a statement and/or question)

_____

_____

_____

_____

Treat

(End the conversation with a statement)

_____

_____

_____

Practice your social exchanges with others frequently
Student-generated social scenario 3

MeNu template

Social scenario

(Create a social scenario about how you interact with your parents after losing computer privileges because of a bad report card.)

Starter

(Start a conversation with an introduction statement)

_____

_____

_____

Main course

(Convey the purpose of your conversation with a statement and/or question)

_____

_____

_____

_____

_____

Treat

(End the conversation with a statement)

_____

_____

_____

Social scenario discussion questions

Review each scenario with your instructor, and answer and discuss the following questions:

- Which scenario best describes you and how you relate to others?

_____

_____

_____

- Did you discover anything new about yourself from this exercise?

_____

_____

_____

- Which scenario was most difficult for you to relate to? Why?

_____

_____

_____

- In this section, which particular areas of social communication were most challenging for you? Why?

_____

_____

_____

- After reviewing the last 15 social scenarios, do you feel more comfortable when interacting socially? Explain.

_____

_____

_____

_____

- Was this section useful? Why or why not?

_____

_____

_____

_____

- How will you implement the MeNu template in future social exchanges? Give three examples.

_____

_____

_____

_____

Chapter 3 summary

In this chapter, following the questionnaire emphasizing communicating effectively, students used the main course MeNu topic examples to review modeled scenarios and respond to social scenario summaries by creating their own social dialogue.

Goal

Students practiced sharing their ideas, thoughts, and interests as they interacted with each other in chapter exercises.

Objective

Students and instructors role-played social exchanges in prescribed social settings, using the MeNu worksheets as a reference.

Favorites and Special MeNu Topics

Produce an effective level of communication

In this chapter: Social conflict

- Produce an effective level of communication
    - Social scenario questionnaire 4: Social conflict
    - Student–instructor feedback sheet: Social scenario questionnaire 4
    - Social conflict MeNu templates 1–5
- Social conflict discussion questions
- Chapter 4 summary

Goal

In this chapter students will identify the value of social communication by completing a social conflict interactive questionnaire and recognizing resolution preferences.

Objective

To maintain a shared conversation with a conversational partner.

Four core concepts to improve social communication:

- **prepare** to communicate socially
- **project** your thoughts, feelings, and ideas appropriately
- **practice** your social exchanges with others frequently
- **produce** an effective level of communication.

Produce an effective level of communication
Social scenario questionnaire 4: Social conflict

There are ten questions in this section. Select answers that best describe how you think you would react in the social scenarios below. You may select "other" to create your own answer.

1. One of your popular classmates invites you to a party at their house. When you arrive, you notice some of the other guests doing illegal drugs. You:

    a. stay at the party, but only interact with those *not* doing drugs

    b. without making any judgments, explain to your classmate hosting the party that you must leave due to the illegal drug activity

    c. want to fit in and engage in a lengthy discussion about the mild versus severe effects of drug use with one of the party guests

    d. call the police to report illegal drug use

    e. other: _____

    _____

2. The game is tied and the referee gives you a penalty for fouling one of your opposing teammates during your basketball game. You don't agree with the referee's call but you don't want to let your teammates down by disputing it. You:

    a. quietly acquiesce in the name of sportsmanship

    b. respectfully agree to disagree with the referee, despite your obvious objection

    c. argue with the referee until he understands your perspective

    d. scream at the referee about his unfair call and stomp off the basketball court, upset

    e. other: _____

    _____

3. You have a part-time job at the deli in town. Sometimes while you're at work your best friend stops by and orders food, but expects to eat for free (because you work there), often leaving without paying for it. You:

    a. explain to your friend that everyone must pay and that you can't make any exceptions, even for friends

    b. offer to loan your friend money for their meal on the condition that they pay you back the money the following day

    c. don't like conflict and give in to your friend, secretly paying for their food yourself

    d. ask your supervisor if you can give your friend food for free

    e. other: _____

    _____

4. A girl in your math class is extremely smart and popular. You'd like to get to know her better, but you're shy and she never seems to acknowledge you at school. You:

    a. practice what you want to say to her until you can bravely ask her a question or if she'd like to study with you sometime

    b. Start making flattering remarks such as: "I think you're smart"

    c. say nothing, but sit next to her every day until she notices you

    d. give up and ignore her because she's in a different social group

    e. other: _____

    _____

5. Your buddy from work borrows money from you and promises to pay you back the following week on payday. After constant reminders from you, they have still not paid you back. You:

    a. realize your friend does not keep their word, and vow never to loan them money again ("lesson learned")

    b. explain to your friend how you feel about not being paid back the money they owe you, and expect them to pay you

    c. verbally hound your friend every payday until they pay you back

    d. tell your friend that you've decided to end your friendship because they are not trustworthy

e. other: _____

_____

6. After getting your driver's license you realize you've become the designated driver for many of your classmates and their errands. As a result, you are running out of gas money needed to drive yourself to and from school. You:

  a. explain the situation to your friends and ask them to share in the gas costs if they'd like you to continue driving them places

  b. say nothing to your friends and ask your parents for more gas money

  c. say nothing and hope that the issue will disappear somehow

  d. abruptly stop driving anyone anywhere, but do not explain why

  e. other: _____

_____

7. You accidentally tell your friend about their surprise birthday party planned for the following weekend, and now they're upset with you for ruining the surprise. You:

  a. explain it was unintentional, immediately apologize to them for your mistake, and ask them to forgive you

  b. ask your friend to attend their party and fake being surprised so as not to embarrass you

  c. say nothing because you don't understand what the big deal is—they were going to find out about their party eventually

  d. announce to everyone at the surprise party that you accidentally told your friend and ruined the surprise

  e. other: _____

_____

8. Your father unexpectedly lost his job. Now your mother is worried about the family finances and decides to cancel the family vacation that you've been looking forward to all year. You:

  a. completely understand their decision and discuss with your parents if you should get a part-time job to help out financially

  b. although upset by this news, calmly tell your parents that you understand their decision under the circumstances, and plan a vacation for a future time

    c. get upset and tell your friends you're poor

    d. say nothing and secretly worry that your father will never get another job

    e. other: _____

    _____

9. You've made plans to hang out at the video arcade with classmates after school, even though you know you have homework and a big test in English the following day. You:

    a. explain your dilemma to your friends and ask for their advice on what you should do

    b. listen to your inner voice that says "go home and study" and skip the arcade altogether

    c. go to the arcade, but are anxious the entire time about the homework that awaits you

    d. go to the arcade and have fun with your friends, telling yourself that school isn't that important to you anyway

    e. other: _____

    _____

10. Your biology teacher just informed you that you will fail biology class unless you receive a C grade or better on your final exam. This upsets you. You:

    a. talk to your biology teacher to see if you have any options to improve your grade

    b. immediately hire a biology tutor to help you study for your biology final exam

    c. plan to repeat the biology class *only* if you fail the final exam

    d. immediately stop attending class all together

    e. other: _____

    _____

Interpreting your questionnaire answers

Total your score. How many a, b, c, d, or e answers did you have? Add the total for each. There are no wrong answers. Information from this exercise reveals your current level of ability to communicate effectively when managing a social conflict. Collectively, answers may vary based on your age, developmental level, and social cognitive ability.

a_____ proficient

b_____ requires practice

c_____ needs assistance

d_____ challenged

e_____ other

The information in this questionnaire answer key is only to be used as a student guide.

Produce an effective level of communication
Student–instructor feedback sheet: Social scenario questionnaire 4

Questionnaire feedback worksheets are used as a method to discuss further each questionnaire answer with your instructor. What was your interpretation of the social conflicts in each scenario? Explain your answers.

What were your answers to each of these questions and why? Explain.

1. One of your popular classmates invites you to a party at their house. When you arrive, you notice some of the other guests doing illegal drugs. You: _____

_____

_____

_____

2. The game is tied and the referee gives you a penalty for fouling one of your opposing teammates during your basketball game. You don't agree with the referee's call but you don't want to let your teammates down by disputing it. You:

_____

_____

_____

3. You have a part-time job at the deli in town. Sometimes while you're at work your best friend stops by and orders food, but expects to eat for free (because you work there), often leaving without paying for it. You: _____

_____

_____

_____

4. A girl in your math class is extremely smart and popular. You'd like to get to know her better, but you're shy and she never seems to acknowledge you at school. You:_____

_____

_____

_____

5. Your buddy from work borrows money from you and promises to pay you back the following week on payday. After constant reminders from you, they have still not paid you back. You:_____

_____

_____

_____

6. After getting your driver's license you realize you've become the designated driver for many of your classmates and their errands. As a result, you are running out of gas money needed to drive yourself to and from school. You:_____

_____

_____

_____

7. You accidentally tell your friend about their surprise birthday party planned for the following weekend, and now they're upset with you for ruining the surprise. You: _____

_____

_____

_____

8. Your father unexpectedly lost his job. Now your mother is worried about the family finances and decides to cancel the family vacation that you've been looking forward to all year. You: _____

_____

_____

_____

9. You've made plans to hang out at the video arcade with classmates after school, even though you know you have homework and a big test in English the following day. You: _____

_____

_____

_____

10. Your biology teacher just informed you that you will fail biology class unless you receive a C grade or better on your final exam. This upsets you. You:_____

_____

_____

_____

Produce an effective level of communication
Social conflict MeNu template 1

Read the social scenario below and create your own social dialogue. Then practice the social dialogue by "role playing" the social scenario with another person.

Social scenario

Your best friend has a crush on a boy in her algebra class. She's confided in you that she intends to become intimate with him soon and has asked for your advice. What do you say to your friend? How do you handle this social issue?

Starter

(Start a conversation with an introduction statement)

_____

_____

_____

Main course

(Convey the purpose of your conversation with a statement and/or question)

_____

_____

_____

_____

Treat

(End the conversation with a statement)

_____

_____

_____

Produce an effective level of communication

Social conflict MeNu template 2

Read the social scenario below and create your own social dialogue. Then practice your social dialogue by "role playing" the social scenario with another person.

Social scenario

A few of your classmates make a plan to cut history class and go to the mall instead. When they ask you to join them, what do you say? What will you do? How do you handle this social situation?

Starter

(Start a conversation with an introduction statement)

_____

_____

_____

Main course

(Convey the purpose of your conversation with a statement and/or question)

_____

_____

_____

_____

Treat

(End the conversation with a statement)

_____

_____

_____

Produce an effective level of communication
Social conflict MeNu template 3

Read the social scenario below and create your own social dialogue. Then practice your social dialogue by "role playing" the social scenario with another person.

Social scenario

Your parents are talking about getting a divorce. Although your father seems overwhelmed, your mother tells you she is relieved by the possibility. Both parents ask for your input on the subject. How do you feel? What do you say to your parents? How do you handle this social and emotional situation?

Starter

(Start a conversation with an introduction statement)

_____

_____

_____

Main course

(Convey the purpose of your conversation with a statement and/or question)

_____

_____

_____

_____

_____

Treat

(End the conversation with a statement)

_____

_____

_____

Produce an effective level of communication
Social conflict MeNu template 4

Read the social scenario below and create your own social dialogue. Then practice your social dialogue by "role playing" the social scenario with another person.

Social scenario

You've noticed several of your friends smoking marijuana (getting high) after school. Although this activity is something you have absolutely no interest in, one of your friends starts to pressure you into trying it with them. How do you handle the peer pressure? What do you say or do?

Starter

(Start a conversation with an introduction statement)

_____

_____

_____

Main course

(Convey the purpose of your conversation with a statement and/or question)

_____

_____

_____

_____

_____

Treat

(End the conversation with a statement)

_____

_____

_____

Produce an effective level of communication
Social conflict MeNu template 5

Read the social scenario below and create your own social dialogue. Then practice your social dialogue by "role playing" the social scenario with another person.

Social scenario

Your brother never came home last night. You know this because you saw him sneak into the house the following morning. He asks you to cover for him so he won't get into trouble with your parents. Your parents ask you if you know anything about the time your brother got in the night before. Knowing the truth will get your brother into trouble, what do you say? How do you address this social situation?

Starter

(Start a conversation with an introduction statement)

_____

_____

_____

Main course

(Convey the purpose of your conversation with a statement and/or question)

_____

_____

_____

_____

_____

Treat

(End the conversation with a statement)

_____

_____

_____

Social conflict discussion questions

Review and discuss each social scenario with your instructor. Answer the following questions:

• Which social scenario was easiest for you to identify with? Explain.

_____

_____

_____

_____

• Describe a specific social scenario that was difficult for you to identify with from Chapter 4? Why was it difficult?

_____

_____

_____

_____

• What kinds of social conflicts have been most difficult for you to address in your own life? Give an example.

_____

_____

_____

_____

• What would you do differently now?

_____

_____

_____

_____

• What did you learn about yourself from this exercise? Explain.

_____

_____

_____

_____

- What information in this exercise will you use to assist you in future social conversations when addressing a conflict? Explain.

_____

_____

_____

_____

Chapter 4 summary

In this chapter, students completed an interactive questionnaire and participated in social conflict scenarios. This was to prepare them for unanticipated future social conflicts, as well as to allow them to practice appropriate resolution preferences.

Goal

Students identified the value of appropriate social communication when addressing social conflicts.

Objective

To maintain a shared conversation with a conversational partner with appropriate dialogue when dealing with an unanticipated social scenario.

Adding Combinations, Sides, and Specials to Your Conversation MeNu

Prepare, project, practice, produce

In this chapter

This chapter emphasizes the importance of social dialoguing when attending social gatherings and other group events while incorporating the four key communication components: **Prepare**, **project**, **practice**, **produce** an effective level of communication.

- Tips and tricks for social conversations
- Movie topic
  - MeNu combination dialogue template
- Sports topic
  - McNu sides/extras dialogue template
- Computer gaming topic
  - MeNu specials dialogue template
- Chomping at the tidbits
- Adding combinations, sides, and specials discussion questions
- Chapter 5 summary

Goal

In this chapter students will practice social dialoguing.

Objective

To display appropriate, frequent, and effective social communication skills.

Four core concepts to improve social communication:

- **prepare** to communicate socially

- **project** your thoughts, feelings, and ideas appropriately

- **practice** your social exchanges with others frequently

- **produce** an effective level of communication.

Tips and tricks for social conversations

Adding combinations, sides, and specials

Whether you are attending a sit-down dinner, holiday meal, or small gathering, engaging in social conversation in these settings typically requires reciprocal conversational skills. Thus, being able to contribute, share, and maintain a connected dialogue on any given topic for a period of time is key.

COMBINATIONS

Combinations are when two people can talk about more than one topic back and forth for a period of time with ease and interest without losing their listener's attention. Combinations are known as a shared conversation. Successfully listening and speaking about multiple topics with your partner takes practice.

SIDES AND EXTRAS

Sides and extras are comments that you can make to add to the topic already being discussed with your conversational partner. These are generally topics that both people have some common knowledge about and are able to speak about freely and naturally.

SPECIALS

Specials are topics that both conversational partners are equally interested in discussing. Specials are usually exciting topics for both conversational partners and are often easier to maintain.

Movie topic
MeNu combination dialogue template

What are MeNu combinations?

MeNu combinations are when you add ideas/opinions to expand a shared conversation while staying on topic.

Read the topic above and create your own social dialogue. Practice this dialogue by role playing this scenario with your instructor.

Starter

(Start a conversation with an introduction statement)

_____

_____

_____

Main course

(Convey the purpose of your conversation with a statement and/or question)

_____

_____

_____

_____

_____

Treat

(End the conversation with a statement)

_____

_____

_____

Sports topic
MeNu sides/extras dialogue template

What are MeNu sides/extras?

MeNu sides/extras are when you add brief and relevant comments or specific facts to an existing conversation.

Read the topic above and create your own social dialogue. Practice this dialogue by role playing this scenario with your instructor.

Starter

(Start a conversation with an introduction statement)

_____

_____

_____

Main course

(Convey the purpose of your conversation with a statement and/or question)

_____

_____

_____

_____

_____

Treat

(End the conversation with a statement)

_____

_____

_____

Computer gaming topic
MeNu specials dialogue template

What are MeNu specials?

MeNu specials are topics that both conversational partners are equally interested in discussing.

Read the topic above and create your own social dialogue. Practice this dialogue by role playing this scenario with your instructor.

Starter

(Start a conversation with an introduction statement)

_____

_____

_____

Main course

(Convey the purpose of your conversation with a statement and/or question)

_____

_____

_____

_____

Treat

(End the conversation with a statement)

_____

_____

_____

Chomping at the tidbits

When you are growing impatient because you have something you want to say, you should:

- be a good listener

- stay on the current speaker's topic

- take turns speaking

- never dominate the conversation

- never interrupt

- be respectful with your comments

- maintain occasional eye contact with the person you are speaking to

- agree and/or disagree respectfully

- not walk away if your conversational partner is still talking.

Food for thought

If you find that you have been the only one talking for more than a few topics, *stop* talking, look at your conversational partner, and say, "I've been doing all the talking. What's new with you?" Listen with interest and let them talk for the same length of time.

Adding combinations, sides, and specials discussion questions

Review the exercises with your instructor and answer the following questions:

• What tips or tricks in Chapter 5 did you learn for future conversations? Explain.

_____

_____

_____

_____

• Give an example of a shared conversation topic.

_____

_____

_____

_____

• What kinds of social "sides and extras" do you typically add to an existing conversation? Give an example.

_____

_____

_____

_____

• What is your favorite topic and how would you weave it into an existing conversation? Explain.

_____

_____

_____

_____

- Give an example of a social scenario where the social "unspoken rules" were broken?

_____

_____

_____

_____

- What information in this exercise will you use to assist you in future social conversations? Explain.

_____

_____

_____

_____

Chapter 5 summary

In this chapter, students recognized the importance of social dialoguing when attending social gatherings and other group events, while keeping in mind the four key communication components. Also in this chapter were tips and tricks for social conversations, chomping at the tidbits, which focused on the unspoken social rules, and MeNu dialoguing templates.

- What are MeNu combinations? Adding ideas/opinions to expand a shared conversation while staying on topic.

- What are MeNu sides/extras? Adding brief and relevant comments or specific facts to an existing conversation.

- What are MeNu specials? Topics that both conversational partners are interested in discussing equally.

Goal

Students practiced social dialoguing.

Objective

To display appropriate, frequent, and effective social communication skills.

MeNu Options

Using social skills with life skills

In this chapter

Students will apply MeNu social communication concepts to articulate their needs in the community, while simultaneously completing life skill tasks.

- Using social skills with life skills
  - Independent life skills ability checklist
- Applying social skills to life skills
  - Skills activities
- MeNu options discussion questions
- Chapter 6 summary

Goal

Students will apply social communication skills and combine them with life skill activities in this exercise.

Objective

To regulate social interactions and complete life skill tasks in the community independently and effectively.

Four core concepts to improve social communication:

- **prepare** to communicate socially
- **project** your thoughts, feelings, and ideas appropriately
- **practice** your social exchanges with others frequently
- **produce** an effective level of communication.

Using social skills with life skills
Independent life skills ability checklist

Select one of the following answers that best describes your current level of ability: Proficient (P), Not proficient (NP), Requires practice (RP), Needs assistance (NA).

    Example: Makes own appointment—P (Proficient)

Self health care skills	P	NP	RP	NA
Is aware of diagnosis	☐	☐	☐	☐
Makes own medical appointments	☐	☐	☐	☐
Makes own dental appointments	☐	☐	☐	☐
Is aware of own health history	☐	☐	☐	☐
Is aware of birth date, current weight, height, age	☐	☐	☐	☐
Has a national insurance card	☐	☐	☐	☐
Has knowledge of family health history	☐	☐	☐	☐
Can take own temperature using thermometer	☐	☐	☐	☐
Is aware of other health conditions (e.g. diabetes, bipolar, seizure disorder)	☐	☐	☐	☐
Requests information from own updated medical file if needed	☐	☐	☐	☐
Administers own medications	☐	☐	☐	☐
Refills own medications at pharmacy	☐	☐	☐	☐
Knows when ill	☐	☐	☐	☐

Personal skills				
Showers or bathes	☐	☐	☐	☐
Shampoos hair	☐	☐	☐	☐
Brushes teeth	☐	☐	☐	☐
Combs hair	☐	☐	☐	☐
Shaves	☐	☐	☐	☐
Gets dressed (selects clothes to wear)	☐	☐	☐	☐
Clips finger/toe nails	☐	☐	☐	☐

	P	NP	RP	NA
Uses alarm clock to get up in the morning	☐	☐	☐	☐
Has haircut	☐	☐	☐	☐
Shops for own clothes	☐	☐	☐	☐
Shops for own shoes	☐	☐	☐	☐

Basic information skills

	P	NP	RP	NA
Knows how to email from a computer	☐	☐	☐	☐
Knows how to text	☐	☐	☐	☐
Uses cell phone	☐	☐	☐	☐
Uses landline telephone	☐	☐	☐	☐
Knows own telephone numbers	☐	☐	☐	☐
Knows own home address	☐	☐	☐	☐
Uses Yellow Pages as a resource	☐	☐	☐	☐
Uses a computer as a resource	☐	☐	☐	☐
Can tell time on numeric clock	☐	☐	☐	☐

Time-management skills/planning

	P	NP	RP	NA
Uses paper calendar	☐	☐	☐	☐
Uses electronic calendar	☐	☐	☐	☐
Uses strategies to manage time	☐	☐	☐	☐
Uses watch/clock to manage time	☐	☐	☐	☐
Maintains daily chore schedule	☐	☐	☐	☐
Follows regular class schedule and routines	☐	☐	☐	☐
Turns in homework on time	☐	☐	☐	☐
Turns in school projects on time	☐	☐	☐	☐
Can multitask chores or school assignments	☐	☐	☐	☐
Can get to and from work/volunteer job on time	☐	☐	☐	☐
Can follow bus schedule	☐	☐	☐	☐

Money skills

	P	NP	RP	NA
Can create monthly budget	☐	☐	☐	☐
Can balance monthly budget	☐	☐	☐	☐
Pays monthly expenses on time	☐	☐	☐	☐
Handles bank transactions:				
Deposits/withdrawals	☐	☐	☐	☐
Debit card	☐	☐	☐	☐
Check writing	☐	☐	☐	☐
Savings account	☐	☐	☐	☐
Credit card purchases/transactions	☐	☐	☐	☐
Online banking skills	☐	☐	☐	☐

Cooking and meal-planning skills

	P	NP	RP	NA
Shops for groceries	☐	☐	☐	☐
Plans meals	☐	☐	☐	☐
Follows recipes (e.g. main course meals and baking)	☐	☐	☐	☐
Cooks and/or prepares nutritious meals (e.g. for self, roommate, family, friends)	☐	☐	☐	☐
Invites a guest over to share a meal they made	☐	☐	☐	☐
Can use independently:				
Stove cook-top (hob)	☐	☐	☐	☐
Oven	☐	☐	☐	☐
Microwave	☐	☐	☐	☐
Dishwasher	☐	☐	☐	☐
Toaster oven	☐	☐	☐	☐
Cutting knives	☐	☐	☐	☐
Hand mixer	☐	☐	☐	☐
Electric mixer	☐	☐	☐	☐
Coffee maker	☐	☐	☐	☐
Electric or hand can opener	☐	☐	☐	☐

	P	NP	RP	NA
Blender	☐	☐	☐	☐
Toaster	☐	☐	☐	☐
Measuring spoons and cups	☐	☐	☐	☐
Barbecue grill (gas or briquettes)	☐	☐	☐	☐
Sets table	☐	☐	☐	☐
Clears table	☐	☐	☐	☐
Washes dishes by hand	☐	☐	☐	☐

Emergency skills

	P	NP	RP	NA
Knows how to turn off main gas line	☐	☐	☐	☐
Knows how to turn off main water line	☐	☐	☐	☐

Can locate and use:

	P	NP	RP	NA
Flashlights	☐	☐	☐	☐
Batteries	☐	☐	☐	☐
First aid kit	☐	☐	☐	☐
Candles and matches	☐	☐	☐	☐
Knows what to do if lost, confused or disoriented	☐	☐	☐	☐

Knows emergency telephone numbers:

	P	NP	RP	NA
Fire department	☐	☐	☐	☐
Police department or 911/999	☐	☐	☐	☐
Gas and electric company	☐	☐	☐	☐
Local plumber	☐	☐	☐	☐
Neighbor or relative	☐	☐	☐	☐

Laundry and household skills

	P	NP	RP	NA
Sorts clothes (by color)	☐	☐	☐	☐
Washes towels and sheets (separately)	☐	☐	☐	☐
Uses washer and dryer (in home)	☐	☐	☐	☐
Uses coin-operated washer/dryer at laundromat	☐	☐	☐	☐

	P	NP	RP	NA
Folds and puts away clothes	☐	☐	☐	☐
Irons clothes	☐	☐	☐	☐
Makes bed	☐	☐	☐	☐
Vacuums and/or sweeps floors	☐	☐	☐	☐
Dusts furniture	☐	☐	☐	☐
Cleans bathrooms (e.g. tub, toilet, sink, floor, mirror)	☐	☐	☐	☐
Waters indoor potted plants	☐	☐	☐	☐
Empties trash	☐	☐	☐	☐
Feeds pet	☐	☐	☐	☐

Outside home task skills

	P	NP	RP	NA
Cuts lawn using lawnmower	☐	☐	☐	☐
Trims shrubs	☐	☐	☐	☐
Waters potted plants	☐	☐	☐	☐
Rakes leaves	☐	☐	☐	☐
Sweeps or shovels	☐	☐	☐	☐
Washes vehicle	☐	☐	☐	☐
Cleans garage	☐	☐	☐	☐

Home repair skills

Minor home repairs:

	P	NP	RP	NA
Changes light bulbs	☐	☐	☐	☐
Changes smoke alarm batteries	☐	☐	☐	☐
Plunges toilet overflow	☐	☐	☐	☐
Climbs ladder	☐	☐	☐	☐
Uses hammer, screwdriver and nails, etc.	☐	☐	☐	☐
Patches wall	☐	☐	☐	☐
Repairs small appliances	☐	☐	☐	☐

Community skills

	P	NP	RP	NA
Uses public transport	☐	☐	☐	☐
Can purchase a transport ticket for:				
Bus	☐	☐	☐	☐
Subway/Underground	☐	☐	☐	☐
Train	☐	☐	☐	☐
Plane	☐	☐	☐	☐
Schedules air travel reservations	☐	☐	☐	☐
Schedules hotel reservations	☐	☐	☐	☐
Uses taxi service	☐	☐	☐	☐
Drives a vehicle	☐	☐	☐	☐
Is aware of pedestrian rules	☐	☐	☐	☐
Uses pay phone	☐	☐	☐	☐
Can read a map	☐	☐	☐	☐
Can use a GPS	☐	☐	☐	☐

Community and social activities

	P	NP	RP	NA
Participates in or attends:				
Movies	☐	☐	☐	☐
Live theater or playhouse	☐	☐	☐	☐
Library	☐	☐	☐	☐
Recreational parks	☐	☐	☐	☐
Clubs (e.g. Boy/Girl Scouts, YMCA, swim club)	☐	☐	☐	☐
Museum	☐	☐	☐	☐
Restaurants	☐	☐	☐	☐
Book store	☐	☐	☐	☐
Shopping	☐	☐	☐	☐
Sporting activities	☐	☐	☐	☐
Community pool	☐	☐	☐	☐
Health club	☐	☐	☐	☐

	P	NP	RP	NA
Video arcades	☐	☐	☐	☐
Music concerts	☐	☐	☐	☐
Art events	☐	☐	☐	☐
Peer camping	☐	☐	☐	☐
Family barbecues	☐	☐	☐	☐
Summer team activities (e.g. swim team, volleyball, baseball)	☐	☐	☐	☐
Winter group trips (e.g. sledding, snowboarding, ice skating)	☐	☐	☐	☐

Social skills

	P	NP	RP	NA
Attends birthday gatherings (e.g. for friend or relative)	☐	☐	☐	☐
Attends holiday parties (e.g. with students, co-workers, friends)	☐	☐	☐	☐
Attends family events (e.g. family reunion, summer weekend trips)	☐	☐	☐	☐
Has friends over for pizza party and video	☐	☐	☐	☐
Has friends over to play group games (poker, board games, card games)	☐	☐	☐	☐
Joins community clubs, church group, support group, health club	☐	☐	☐	☐
Participates in team sport (e.g. basketball)	☐	☐	☐	☐
Organizes a party or event (e.g. bowling, movie)	☐	☐	☐	☐
Plans family vacation (locally, internationally)	☐	☐	☐	☐
Plans overnight outing with peer group (e.g. camping, skiing)	☐	☐	☐	☐
Joins community theater group	☐	☐	☐	☐
Joins religious school peer groups	☐	☐	☐	☐
Joins school clubs (e.g. student council, cheerleading)	☐	☐	☐	☐
Attends school football games or dances	☐	☐	☐	☐
Attends formal dances or graduation ceremonies	☐	☐	☐	☐
Joins after school club (e.g. art, track, computer media)	☐	☐	☐	☐
Attends school event (e.g. dances, football, basketball, soccer games)	☐	☐	☐	☐
Participates in school fundraising (e.g. car wash, bake sale)	☐	☐	☐	☐

Interpreting your independent life skills ability checklist answers

Total your score. How many P, NP, RP, or NA answers did you have? Write the total for each. There are no wrong answers. Information from this exercise reveals your current level of ability in independent life skills, as well as which life skills require more practice. Collectively, answers may vary based on your age, developmental level, and social cognitive ability.

P _____ proficient

NP_____ not proficient

RP_____ requires practice

NA_____ needs assistance

The information in this questionnaire answer key is only to be used as a student guide.

Applying social skills to life skills

Skill building is a process. In this chapter students will be integrating social skill MeNu techniques and strategies outlined in Chapters 1 through 5, with real-life skill experiences. The goal is to improve social interactions with those in the community, while practicing independent life skill tasks. Based on results from the independent life skills ability checklist, using the MeNu template four-step process, students will design and complete individualized task activities concentrating on their own specific areas of need.

Each MeNu task activity has a four-step process:

- The first-step McNu template: the student identifies a life skill task, task set-up, social goal for the task, and a "mock" dialogue to be used as a reference or review before completing the actual life skill task independently.

- The second-step MeNu template: after completing the task independently, the student records the social dialogue they actually used when completing their life skill task.

- The third-step MeNu template: the student uses a task checklist to ensure that the task set-up, social goal, and life skill task itself were completed.

- The fourth-step MeNu template: the student uses a feedback questionnaire to measure their life skill task performance and proficiency for that particular task.

Apply the four-step MeNu template process for each of the following social and life skill sections: Self health care, Personal, Basic information, Time management, Money, Cooking and meal planning, Emergency, Laundry and household, Outside home, Home repair, Community, and Social skill building.

All four MeNu steps should be reviewed and discussed with an instructor following the completion of each life skill task.

Doctor's appointment
Self health care skill

Task: Schedule a doctor's appointment for yourself.

Task set-up: Create a list of your current doctors. Write down their contact information such as names, addresses, phone numbers, and office hours.

Note: Most people have an established relationship with some type of doctor. If you do not, research specialties that have expertise in the area in which you require assistance.

Social goal: Interact with the doctor's office staff to schedule an appointment for yourself.

Food for thought

Think of the MeNu as a social reference on how to:

Starter

Start a conversation with an introduction statement
Example: "Hello, my name is Cindy Smith."

Main course

Convey the purpose of your conversation with a statement and/or question
Example: "I would like to schedule an appointment to see Dr. Jones regarding my annual physical exam. Can you help me schedule that appointment? Tuesday and Thursday afternoons work best for me."

Treat

End the conversation with a statement
Example: "Thank you for your help."

Complete task now!

Doctor's appointment
MeNu template

(Complete task template by recounting the social dialogue used in task activity)

Starter
(Write in the starter you used in this task)

_____

_____

_____

Main course
(Write in the main course you used in this task)

_____

_____

_____

_____

_____

Treat
(Write in the treat you used in this task)

_____

_____

_____

Doctor's appointment
Checklist

Please answer each of the following checklist questions.

Did you complete the task set up? ☐

Did you complete the task? ☐

Did you accomplish the social goal? ☐

Doctor's appointment
Student feedback questionnaire

Answer each of the following questions and explain each answer.

What was the goal of this task?

_____

_____

_____

How difficult was this task?

_____

_____

_____

Were there any social challenges?

_____

_____

_____

What did you learn?

_____

_____

_____

Could you perform this task independently next time?

_____

_____

_____

When will you perform this task again?

_____

_____

_____

How would you prepare?

_____

_____

_____

Do you have any thoughts, concerns, or questions about this task?

_____

_____

_____

Dental appointment
Self health care skill

Task: Schedule a dental appointment for yourself.

Task set-up: Refer to the contact information you have for your dentist such as name, address, phone number, office hours, and their emergency office number.

Note: Most people have an established relationship with some type of dentist. If you do not, research specialties that have expertise in the area in which you require assistance.

Social goal: Interact with dental office staff to schedule an appointment for yourself.

Food for thought

Think of the MeNu as a social reference on how to:

Starter

Start a conversation with an introduction statement
Example: "Hello, my name is Andy White."

Main course

Convey the purpose of your conversation with a statement and/or question
Example: "I would like to schedule an appointment to see Dr. Wada regarding my front tooth. I'm having a lot of pain chewing and I'd like to see the dentist as soon as possible. Can you help me?"

Treat

End the conversation with a statement
Example: "Thank you for your help."

Complete task now!

Dental appointment
MeNu template

(Complete task template by recounting the social dialogue used in task activity)

Starter

(Write in the starter you used in this task)

_____

_____

_____

Main course

(Write in the main course you used in this task)

_____

_____

_____

_____

_____

Treat

(Write in the treat you used in this task)

_____

_____

_____

Dental appointment
Checklist

Please answer each of the following checklist questions.

Did you complete the task set-up? ☐

Did you complete the task? ☐

Did you accomplish the social goal? ☐

Dental appointment
Student feedback questionnaire

Answer each of the following questions and explain each answer.

What was the goal of this task?

_____

_____

_____

How difficult was this task?

_____

_____

_____

Were there any social challenges?

_____

_____

_____

What did you learn?

_____

_____

_____

Could you perform this task independently next time?

_____

_____

_____

When will you perform this task again?

_____

_____

_____

How would you prepare?

_____

_____

_____

Do you have any thoughts, concerns, or questions about this task?

_____

_____

_____

Other self health care tasks

Complete each of the following tasks independently:

- Discuss diagnosis with medical doctors when necessary. Provide accurate and relevant medical information. Ask questions, share any concerns, take notes. Identify psychological, emotional, or physical issues.

- On your next doctor's visit, fully complete a medical or dental personal information form (birth date, current weight, height, age, ailments, medical family history, medication, and dosage).

- Administer own medication(s) as directed.

- Refill own prescribed medication(s) at pharmacy before old prescription is empty.

- Discuss with doctor any substance or addiction issues.

Getting ready for school
Personal skill

Task: Get up and ready for school independently.

Task set-up: Set alarm clock, prepare clothes, lunch, and backpack with homework and/or school supplies the night before. In the morning, get up using alarm clock, shower, shampoo hair, brush teeth, comb hair (shave if needed), get dressed, make and eat breakfast. Gather school belongings and backpack.

Note: Each student is different in their ability to manage themselves and time effectively. To accomplish this task independently, weekend practice is encouraged to determine how much time is needed (estimate: one hour).

Social goal: Pleasantly greet and interact with parent(s) or sibling(s) before school.

Food for thought

Think of the MeNu as a social reference on how to:

Starter

Start a conversation with an introduction statement
Example: "Good morning, Mom/Dad."

Main course

Convey the purpose of your conversation with a statement and/or question
Example: "I was wondering, will you be picking me up after school today or should I plan to walk home?"

Treat

End the conversation with a statement
Example: "See you after school."

Complete task now!

Getting ready for school
MeNu template

(Complete task template by recounting the social dialogue used in task activity)

Starter

(Write in the starter you used in this task)

_____

_____

_____

Main course

(Write in the main course you used in this task)

_____

_____

_____

_____

_____

Treat

(Write in the treat you used in this task)

_____

_____

_____

Getting ready for school
Checklist

Please answer each of the following checklist questions.

Did you complete the task set-up? ☐

Did you complete the task? ☐

Did you accomplish the social goal? ☐

Getting ready for school
Student feedback questionnaire

Answer each of the following questions and explain each answer.

What was the goal of this task?

_____

_____

_____

How difficult was this task?

_____

_____

_____

Were there any social challenges?

_____

_____

_____

What did you learn?

_____

_____

_____

Could you perform this task independently next time?

_____

_____

_____

When will you perform this task again?

_____

_____

_____

How would you prepare?

_____

_____

_____

Do you have any thoughts, concerns, or questions about this task?

_____

_____

_____

Haircut
Personal skill

Task: Make an appointment to get a haircut.

Task set-up: If you don't already use a particular salon or barber shop, reference the Yellow Pages and/or internet for one near you. Call and schedule a haircut appointment with one of their beauticians or barbers for a mutually convenient time and date (for you and them).

Note: Some students have tactile or sensory defensive issues and sometimes a haircut can trigger a sensory overload, resulting in a meltdown. Extra time at the least busy time of day may work best.

Social goal: Interact pleasantly with receptionist when scheduling haircut appointment.

Food for thought

Think of the MeNu as a social reference on how to:

Starter

Start a conversation with an introduction statement
Example: "Hi, how are you? I'm calling to make a haircut appointment for myself."

Main course

Convey the purpose of your conversation with a statement and/or question
Example: "Do you have any openings today or tomorrow? I just need a trim. What do you charge for a trim, and how long do you think that would take?"

Treat

End the conversation with a statement
Example: "OK, thanks for the information. See you soon."

Complete task now!

Haircut
MeNu template

(Complete task template by recounting the social dialogue used in task activity)

Starter

(Write in the starter you used in this task)

_____

_____

_____

Main course

(Write in the main course you used in this task)

_____

_____

_____

_____

_____

Treat

(Write in the treat you used in this task)

_____

_____

_____

Haircut
Checklist

Please answer each of the following checklist questions.

Did you complete the task set-up? ☐

Did you complete the task? ☐

Did you accomplish the social goal? ☐

Haircut
Student feedback questionnaire

Answer each of the following questions and explain each answer.

What was the goal of this task?

_____

_____

_____

How difficult was this task?

_____

_____

_____

Were there any social challenges?

_____

_____

_____

What did you learn?

_____

_____

_____

Could you perform this task independently next time?

_____

_____

_____

When will you perform this task again?

_____

_____

_____

How would you prepare?

_____

_____

_____

Do you have any thoughts, concerns, or questions about this task?

_____

_____

_____

Other personal skill tasks

Complete each of the following tasks independently:

- Shop for own clothes. Demonstrate ability to price and purchase appropriately.
- Shop for own shoes. Demonstrate ability to know when new shoes are necessary.
- Shop for personal items: toothpaste, hairspray, shaving cream, shampoo, soap, etc.
- Exhibit ability to appropriately answer and use telephone.

Text messaging and email
Basic information skill

Task: Text (or email) a classmate to confirm homework assignment.

Task set-up: Using a cell phone (or computer), text or type a question to clarify or confirm a homework assignment with a classmate. In the body of the message include starter, main course, and treat statements as you interact back and forth.

Note: Each student is different in their ability to articulate their thoughts and/or communicate effectively. To accomplish this task independently, practice "texting" or "emailing" your parents with similar questions or requests, using the MeNu template as a protocol, prior to completing this task.

Social goal: Request information needed while interacting appropriately with classmate regarding class assignment.

Food for thought

Think of the MeNu as a social reference on how to:

Starter

Start a conversation with an introduction statement
Example: "Hi there, it's me, Samantha. I have a question for you regarding our math homework."

Main course

Convey the purpose of your conversation with a statement and/or question
Example: "Do you know what our algebra homework assignment is? I didn't write it down in class today and I wanted to get started on it."

Treat

End the conversation with a statement
Example: "OK, thanks for the information. See you tomorrow in class."

Complete task now!

Text messaging and email
MeNu template

(Complete task template by recounting the social dialogue used in task activity)

Starter
(Write in the starter you used in this task)

_____

_____

_____

Main course
(Write in the main course you used in this task)

_____

_____

_____

_____

_____

Treat
(Write in the treat you used in this task)

_____

_____

_____

Text messaging and email
Checklist

Please answer each of the following checklist questions.

Did you complete the task set-up? ☐

Did you complete the task? ☐

Did you accomplish the social goal? ☐

Text messaging and email
Student feedback questionnaire

Answer each of the following questions and explain each answer.

What was the goal of this task?

_____

_____

_____

How difficult was this task?

_____

_____

_____

Were there any social challenges?

_____

_____

_____

What did you learn?

_____

_____

_____

Could you perform this task independently next time?

_____

_____

_____

When will you perform this task again?

_____

_____

_____

How would you prepare?

_____

_____

_____

Do you have any thoughts, concerns, or questions about this task?

_____

_____

_____

Yellow Pages as a resource
Basic information skill

Task: Use the Yellow Pages as a resource to locate a post office.

Task set-up: Using the Yellow Pages, determine the nearest post office (to your residence) and call them to clarify their hours of operation.

Note: Each student is different in their ability to navigate through resource information. Most cities provide their residents and businesses with a telephone directory (book). This is a book listing telephone subscribers. White pages list personal information alphabetically (name, address, phone number). Yellow pages list various business and service information categorized by section from A to Z. The telephone book often includes information relating to governmental agencies, maps, postal codes, and emergency management information (emergency service numbers, hospitals, doctors, etc.). The telephone book can also be found on the internet.

Social goal: Request information needed from postal employee.

Food for thought

Think of the MeNu as a social reference on how to:

Starter

Start a conversation with an introduction statement
Example: "Hello. My name is Mary and I live on East San Francisco."

Main course

Convey the purpose of your conversation with a statement and/or question
Example: "I'm trying to locate the post office closest to my house. Can you tell me if your post office is closest to 555 E. San Francisco Street? Also, what are the opening hours Monday to Saturday?"

Treat

End the conversation with a statement
Example: "OK, thanks for the information. I appreciate it."

Complete task now!

Yellow Pages as a resource
MeNu template

(Complete task template by recounting the social dialogue used in task activity)

Starter

(Write in the starter you used in this task)

_____

_____

_____

Main course

(Write in the main course you used in this task)

_____

_____

_____

_____

_____

Treat

(Write in the treat you used in this task)

_____

_____

_____

Yellow Pages as a resource
Checklist

Please answer each of the following checklist questions.

Did you complete the task set-up? ☐

Did you complete the task? ☐

Did you accomplish the social goal? ☐

Yellow Pages as a resource
Student feedback questionnaire

Answer each of the following questions and explain each answer.

What was the goal of this task?

_____

_____

_____

How difficult was this task?

_____

_____

_____

Were there any social challenges?

_____

_____

_____

What did you learn?

_____

_____

_____

Could you perform this task independently next time?

_____

_____

_____

When will you perform this task again?

_____

_____

_____

How would you prepare?

_____

_____

_____

Do you have any thoughts, concerns, or questions about this task?

_____

_____

_____

Other basic skill tasks

Complete each of the following tasks independently:

- Use a computer to email a letter.
- Use a cell phone to call a parent.
- Use a landline telephone to call a relative.
- Memorize your own home address and phone numbers and call home from a pay telephone.
- Use the Yellow Pages as a resource to find a local restaurant for dinner.
- Use the internet as a resource to find the address of the local library or bookstore.
- Use a map to get from home from a local bookstore.
- Register to vote if 18 or older.
- Write a thank-you note by hand and mail it.
- Buy and read a newspaper or magazine.
- Apply for a library card.

Calendar scheduling
Time-management skill

Task: To become organized by managing own appointments, school assignments, and overall daily schedule using a monthly calendar.

Task set-up: Using a paper or electronic computerized calendar, make your monthly schedule to include class assignment due dates, homework, class projects, personal appointments, household chores, sporting activities, and club meetings.

Note: Time management can be difficult for any student with executive functioning issues. To improve this skill, practice using time-management techniques by scheduling weekend activities and events by the hour and/or 30-minute intervals to your calendar. Include dates and times for each event, activity, school assignment, or appointment in your monthly calendar.

Social goal: Communicate with parents, peers, teachers, friends, and classmates to confirm information and/or schedule activities.

Food for thought

Think of the MeNu as a social reference on how to:

Starter

Start a conversation with an introduction statement
Example: "Dad/Mom, I need your help with something."

Main course

Convey the purpose of your conversation with a statement and/or question
Example: "I'm making a monthly calendar of all of my activities and appointments so I can be more organized and responsible. Can you tell me when my next orthodontist and haircut appointments are scheduled for? What other appointments do I have scheduled this month?"

Treat

End the conversation with a statement
Example: "Thanks for your help."

Complete task now!

Calendar scheduling
MeNu template

(Complete task template by recounting the social dialogue used in task activity)

Starter

(Write in the starter you used in this task)

_____

_____

_____

Main course

(Write in the main course you used in this task)

_____

_____

_____

_____

_____

Treat

(Write in the treat you used in this task)

_____

_____

_____

Calendar scheduling
Checklist

Please answer each of the following checklist questions.

Did you complete the task set-up? ☐

Did you complete the task? ☐

Did you accomplish the social goal? ☐

Calendar scheduling
Student feedback questionnaire

Answer each of the following questions and explain each answer.

What was the goal of this task?

_____

_____

_____

How difficult was this task?

_____

_____

_____

Were there any social challenges?

_____

_____

_____

What did you learn?

_____

_____

_____

Could you perform this task independently next time?

_____

_____

_____

When will you perform this task again?

_____

_____

_____

How would you prepare?

_____

_____

_____

Do you have any thoughts, concerns, or questions about this task?

_____

_____

_____

Complete and turn homework in on time
Time-management skill

Task: To complete and manage own homework assignments; turn in work to teachers on time.

Task set-up: Using calendar system, organize and manage your schoolwork and homework due dates.

Note: Homework management can be difficult for any student with executive functioning issues. To improve this skill, complete homework assignments in advance of their scheduled due date. This allows time to review your work and make any necessary changes.

Social goal: Communicate with teachers regarding exact due dates for homework assignments.

Food for thought

Think of the MeNu as a social reference on how to:

Starter

Start a conversation with an introduction statement
Example: "Hi, Miss Greene, I have a homework question."

Main course

Convey the purpose of your conversation with a statement and/or question
Example: "I'm trying to become more organized with my homework management. Can you please tell me what homework is due this week? I'm trying to coordinate the assignment with homework from my other classes."

Treat

End the conversation with a statement
Example: "Thanks for your help."

Complete task now!

Complete and turn homework in on time
MeNu template

(Complete task template by recounting the social dialogue used in task activity)

Starter
(Write in the starter you used in this task)

_____

_____

_____

Main course
(Write in the main course you used in this task)

_____

_____

_____

_____

_____

Treat
(Write in the treat you used in this task)

_____

_____

_____

Complete and turn homework in on time
Checklist

Please answer each of the following checklist questions.

Did you complete the task-set up? ☐

Did you complete the task? ☐

Did you accomplish the social goal? ☐

Complete and turn homework in on time
Student feedback questionnaire

Answer each of the following questions and explain each answer.

What was the goal of this task?

_____

_____

_____

How difficult was this task?

_____

_____

_____

Were there any social challenges?

_____

_____

_____

What did you learn?

_____

_____

_____

Could you perform this task independently next time?

_____

_____

_____

When will you perform this task again?

_____

_____

_____

How would you prepare?

_____

_____

_____

Do you have any thoughts, concerns, or questions about this task?

_____

_____

_____

Other time-management skill tasks

Complete each of the following tasks independently:

- Create chart to manage completion of household chores.
- Prioritize schoolwork assignments according to due dates.
- Make a chart to categorize weekly "to do" list.
- Plan how to get to and from work/volunteer job on time.
- Follow a bus schedule to the grocery store and back home.
- Set short- and long-term personal goals with benchmarks.
- Plan a social outing with a friend and coordinate the time frame, location, and activity with them.
- Recognize and respond appropriately to a time-sensitive issue.
- Pay a household bill before its due date.
- Check out and return a library book or video rental before its due date.

Bank transaction
Money skill

Task: Open up a checking (current) and/or savings account at your local bank.

Task set-up: Visit local banks to determine where you will be banking. Research "bank accounts" on the internet to familiarize yourself with the process and variety of banking options prior to opening your bank account.

Note: A savings account accrues interest on money that is deposited. A checking (current) account allows the account holder to write checks. An Automatic Teller Machine or ATM allows the account holder to deposit or withdrawal money from their bank account.

Social goal: Interact with banker to open up bank account.

Food for thought

Think of the MeNu as a social reference on how to:

Starter

Start a conversation with an introduction statement
Example: "Hello, my name is Joe Black."

Main course

Convey the purpose of your conversation with a statement and/or question
Example: "I would like to open up a checking account. Can you help me do that? Before we get started, can you explain what types of checking accounts you offer here?"

Treat

End the conversation with a statement
Example: "Thank you for your help."

Complete task now!

Bank transaction
MeNu template

(Complete task template by recounting the social dialogue used in task activity)

Starter
(Write in the starter you used in this task)

_____

_____

_____

Main course
(Write in the main course you used in this task)

_____

_____

_____

_____

Treat
(Write in the treat you used in this task)

_____

_____

_____

Bank transaction
Checklist

Please answer each of the following checklist questions.

Did you complete the task set-up? ☐

Did you complete the task? ☐

Did you accomplish the social goal? ☐

Bank transaction
Student feedback questionnaire

Answer each of the following questions and explain each answer.

What was the goal of this task?

_____

_____

_____

How difficult was this task?

_____

_____

_____

Were there any social challenges?

_____

_____

_____

What did you learn?

_____

_____

_____

Could you perform this task independently next time?

_____

_____

_____

When will you perform this task again?

_____

_____

_____

How would you prepare?

_____

_____

_____

Do you have any thoughts, concerns, or questions about this task?

_____

_____

_____

Monthly budget
Money skill

Task: To create a monthly budget.

Task set-up: Write down your monthly net (after taxes) income. Then make a list of your monthly expenses. Estimate projected expenses if necessary. Research a budget and/or finance book or "monthly budget" using the internet for household budget templates. Review and select one that best suits your needs. You may choose to use the example on the next page.

Note: Creating a monthly budget can be difficult. Balancing your monthly finances when you have different sources of income (and dates that you receive them) takes practice. Use your monthly calendar to help organize what's due when. Pay your bills prior to their due date, allowing mail travel time.

Social goal: Interact with cable service to negotiate the best price for a basic cable plan.

Food for thought

Think of the MeNu as a social reference on how to:

Starter

Start a conversation with an introduction statement
Example: "Hello, my name is John White, and I would like some information about your cable plans."

Main course

Convey the purpose of your conversation with a statement and/or question
Example: "What are your basic cable options? Are you offering any specials right now? I'm trying to get the best price for what I need. Can you handle any change I make to my plan over the phone?"

Treat

End the conversation with a statement
Example: "Thank you for your help."

Complete task now!

Monthly budget
Budget example

	$
Total monthly income after taxes $	_____
Total monthly expenses $	_____
(Subtract expenses from income)	_____
Monthly expenses	_____
Housing expenses	_____
Mortgage or rent	_____
Utilities (gas and electric usage)	_____
Home telephone	_____
Water usage	_____
Garbage removal	_____
Miscellaneous home repairs and improvement	_____
Home insurance	_____
Other	_____
Living expenses	_____
Food	_____
Eating out	_____
Housekeeping service	_____
Laundromat	_____
Dry cleaning	_____
Other	_____
Personal care expenses	_____
Clothing	_____
Shoes	_____
Haircuts	_____
Shampoo, conditioner, toothpaste, etc.	_____
Vitamins and minerals, etc.	_____
Other	_____

$

Health expenses _____

Medical insurance _____

Dental insurance _____

Life insurance _____

Pharmacy expenses _____

Over-the-counter medicines _____

Co-payments to doctor _____

Co-payments to dentist _____

Health club fee _____

Other _____

Transportation _____

Vehicle payment _____

Gas/fuel _____

Vehicle insurance _____

Vehicle licensing/registration _____

Vehicle maintenance/repairs _____

Parking fees _____

Public transportation fees _____

Other _____

Entertainment _____

Cable television _____

Internet service _____

Cell phone _____

Movies _____

Plays _____

Music concerts or clubs _____

DVD rentals _____

Live sporting events _____

Other _____

$

Recreation

Magazine subscriptions

Newspaper subscriptions

Books

Music

Community classes (dance, music, art)

Religious organization fee

Community organization fee

Other

Miscellaneous expenses

Birthday/holiday/special occasion gifts

Flowers

Plants

Pet expenses

Other

Financial

Savings

Banking fees

Pension

Taxes

Other

Monthly budget
MeNu template

(Complete task template by recounting the social dialogue used in task activity)

Starter

(Write in the starter you used in this task)

_____

_____

_____

Main course

(Write in the main course you used in this task)

_____

_____

_____

_____

_____

Treat

(Write in the treat you used in this task)

_____

_____

_____

Monthly budget
Checklist

Please answer each of the following checklist questions.

Did you complete the task set-up? ☐

Did you complete the task? ☐

Did you accomplish the social goal? ☐

Monthly budget
Student feedback questionnaire

Answer each of the following questions and explain each answer.

What was the goal of this task?

_____

_____

_____

How difficult was this task?

_____

_____

_____

Were there any social challenges?

_____

_____

_____

What did you learn?

_____

_____

_____

Could you perform this task independently next time?

_____

_____

_____

When will you perform this task again?

_____

_____

_____

How would you prepare?

_____

_____

_____

Do you have any thoughts, concerns, or questions about this task?

_____

_____

_____

Other money and life skill tasks

Complete each of the following tasks independently:

- Demonstrate the ability to understand the value and purpose of money.
- Demonstrate the ability to make change using bills and coins.
- Pay a monthly expense on time.
- Utilize an ATM card to purchase a grocery item.
- Write a check to pay a household bill.
- Make a credit card purchase to buy a necessity item.
- Understand and utilize the purpose of online internet banking.
- Understand how to use a debit card.
- Calculate the tax and/or tip towards a restaurant bill.

Shopping
Cooking and meal-planning skill

Task: Shopping for items needed to make an avocado dip.

Task set-up: Visit your local shops as many times as necessary to decide where you will be shopping. If sensory issues exist, add extra visits prior to your actual shopping excursion to determine the best time and day of the week to support this outing (e.g. less crowded, less noisy). Familiarize yourself with where the market is located and where items are located and setup inside.

Shopping list and recipe:

1 garlic clove	1 tsp (teaspoon) of chilli power
2 ripe avocados	½ tsp (teaspoon) paprika
1 tbsp (tablespoon) olive oil	1 tsp (teaspoon) of black pepper
1 tbsp (tablespoon) lemon juice	1 bag of white corn tortilla chips

Social goal: Ask for help locating an item on your shopping list.

Food for thought

Think of the MeNu as a social reference on how to:

Starter

Start a conversation with an introduction statement
Example: "Excuse me; can you please help me find something I'm looking for?"

Main course

Convey the purpose of your conversation with a statement and/or question
Example: "I'm making an avocado dip and can't find where the avocados are located. Can you please show me where they are?"

Treat

End the conversation with a statement
Example: "Thank you for your help."

Complete task now!

Shopping
MeNu template

(Complete task template by recounting the social dialogue used in task activity)

Starter

(Write in the starter you used in this task)

_____

_____

_____

Main course

(Write in the main course you used in this task)

_____

_____

_____

_____

_____

Treat

(Write in the treat you used in this task)

_____

_____

_____

Shopping
Checklist

Please answer each of the following checklist questions.

Did you complete the task set-up? ☐

Did you complete the task? ☐

Did you accomplish the social goal? ☐

Shopping
Student feedback questionnaire

Answer each of the following questions and explain each answer.

What was the goal of this task?

_____

_____

_____

How difficult was this task?

_____

_____

_____

Were there any social challenges?

_____

_____

_____

What did you learn?

_____

_____

_____

Could you perform this task independently next time?

_____

_____

_____

When will you perform this task again?

_____

_____

_____

How would you prepare?

_____

_____

_____

Do you have any thoughts, concerns, or questions about this task?

_____

_____

_____

Preparing dip
Cooking and meal-planning skill

Task: Prepare avocado dip using ingredients collected from shopping task.

Task set-up: Gather all ingredients.

1 garlic clove	1 tsp (teaspoon) of chilli power
2 ripe avocados	½ tsp (teaspoon) paprika
1 tbsp (tablespoon) olive oil	1 tsp (teaspoon) of black pepper
1 tbsp (tablespoon) lemon juice	1 bag of white corn tortilla chips

Peel, then crush garlic clove and place into bowl. Add all other recipe ingredients and mash with fork to give a rough-textured dip. Serve with corn tortilla chips. Enjoy!

Social goal: Invite someone in your family to share chips and dip with you.

Food for thought

Think of the MeNu as a social reference on how to:

Starter

Start a conversation with an introduction statement
Example: "Hey, Dad, I just finished making a new avocado dip recipe. Would you like to try some with me?"

Main course

Convey the purpose of your conversation with a statement and/or question
Example: "I'm serving the dip with corn chips. What do you think of the dip? Do you like it?"

Treat

End the conversation with a statement
Example: "Thanks for tasting my dip, Dad."

Complete task now!

Preparing dip
MeNu template

(Complete task template by recounting the social dialogue used in task activity)

Starter

(Write in the starter you used in this task)

_____

_____

_____

Main course

(Write in the main course you used in this task)

_____

_____

_____

_____

_____

Treat

(Write in the treat you used in this task)

_____

_____

_____

Preparing dip
Checklist

Please answer each of the following checklist questions.

Did you complete the task set-up? ☐

Did you complete the task? ☐

Did you accomplish the social goal? ☐

Preparing dip
Student feedback questionnaire

Answer each of the following questions and explain each answer.

What was the goal of this task?

_____

_____

_____

How difficult was this task?

_____

_____

_____

Were there any social challenges?

_____

_____

_____

What did you learn?

_____

_____

_____

Could you perform this task independently next time?

_____

_____

_____

When will you perform this task again?

_____

_____

_____

How would you prepare?

_____

_____

_____

Do you have any thoughts, concerns, or questions about this task?

_____

_____

_____

Other cooking and meal-planning tasks

Complete each of the following tasks independently:

- Grocery shop for the entire week.
- Pay for weekly groceries with check or debit card.
- Put away and stored groceries properly. Organize staple foods, freezer foods, refrigerated foods.
- Sanitize food preparation areas (counters and tables) before cooking.
- Follow and complete a four-step recipe. Read and understand label contents. Use measuring utensils accurately. Use cutting knives and cooking ware safely.
- Prepare a three-course meal for at least four people.
- Bake or make a dessert, following a recipe.
- Invite friends over for a meal you've prepared.
- Set a table using table cloth, plates, glasses, napkins, utensils.
- Remove dirty dishes from table, wash and dry dirty dishes, and put away.

Contact local gas and electric company
Emergency skill

Task: Make a list of the emergency service providers in your area.

Task set-up: Create a list of local emergency service providers. Write down their contact information such as names, addresses, phone numbers, and office hours. Make sure this list is visible and easy for you to locate at all times.

Note: If you don't have a list of local service providers that you've used in the past, such as plumbers, electricians, or handymen, use other resources and recommendations such as local telephone book, internet, neighbor, friend, or family member.

Social goal: Call your local gas and/or electric company and inform them of a power outage in your home. If they are already aware of the outage, politely request assistance and/or information to determine when the gas/electrical power will return to your home.

Food for thought

Think of the MeNu as a social reference on how to:

Starter

Start a conversation with an introduction statement
Example: "Hello, my name is Sandy Smith and I'm calling to let you know that my power is out."

Main course

Convey the purpose of your conversation with a statement and/or question
Example: "My address is 555 Main Street, and I've been without power for two hours now. Can you please send one of your technicians to my home to determine the problem?"

Treat

End the conversation with a statement
Example: "Thank you for your help."

Complete task now!

Contact local gas and electric company
MeNu template

(Complete task template by recounting the social dialogue used in task activity)

Starter

(Write in the starter you used in this task)

_____

_____

_____

Main course

(Write in the main course you used in this task)

_____

_____

_____

_____

_____

Treat

(Write in the treat you used in this task)

_____

_____

_____

Contact local gas and electric company
Checklist

Please answer each of the following checklist questions.

Did you complete the task set-up? ☐

Did you complete the task? ☐

Did you accomplish the social goal? ☐

Contact local gas and electric company
Student feedback questionnaire

Answer each of the following questions and explain each answer.

What was the goal of this task?

_____

_____

_____

How difficult was this task?

_____

_____

_____

Were there any social challenges?

_____

_____

_____

What did you learn?

_____

_____

_____

Could you perform this task independently next time?

_____

_____

_____

When will you perform this task again?

_____

_____

_____

How would you prepare?

_____

_____

_____

Do you have any thoughts, concerns, or questions about this task?

_____

_____

_____

Other emergency and life skill tasks

Complete each of the following tasks independently:

- Demonstrate the ability to understand *when* to contact someone from your emergency number list.

- Create a list of people you can contact in case of an emergency:
  - neighbor's name and numbers
  - nearby relative's name and numbers
  - local emergency family shelter (name, number, address/location).

- Fill an emergency backpack with items to take with you in case of an emergency:
  - extra prescribed medications
  - health insurance card and information, and $50 cash (small bills)
  - flashlight, batteries, candles, matches, hand-held radio
  - one complete change of clothes including shoes, hat, coat.

- Create a safety skills checklist and practice the following:
  - exit a building during a fire alarm (practice without alarm)
  - cross a busy intersection
  - report an unlawful act being witnessed
  - understand appropriate behavior when/if interacting with a law enforcement officer.

Laundromat
Laundry or household skill

Task: Wash, dry, fold, and put away laundry.

Task set-up: Visit several local laundromats to decide which one you will use and confirm their hours of operation. Clarify how much it will cost to wash one load (using the washer) and dry that same load (using the dryer). Determine what type of coin(s) each machine requires (e.g. washer may require eight quarters per load, while dryer may require ten quarters per load). If auditory sensory issues exist, determine the best time and day of the week to support this outing (e.g. less crowded, less noisy machines).

Note: Look at every clothing label to confirm washing instructions. Some may say "machine washable," or "wash with like colors." Others might say "hand wash," "wash in cold water," "hang dry," or "dry clean only," etc. For this exercise you will look for "machine washable" or words similar to this. Practice sorting clothes by color and type. Example: like-colored towels are typically washed together as one load in HOT water (you will select the water temperature on the washer before you start). Dark-colored clothing is typically washed together in COLD water. White or light-colored clothing is typically washed in WARM water. If you are not sure which water temperature you should use, select the warm water setting. When clothes are dry, fold and pack to bring home (using laundry basket or laundry bag). Hint: folding clothes when warm reduces wrinkles.

Social goal: Interact with others at the laundromat.

Food for thought

Think of the MeNu as a social reference on how to:

Starter

Start a conversation with an introduction statement
Example: "Hi, this is my first time using these washers and dryers."

Main course

Convey the purpose of your conversation with a statement and/or question
Example: "It's all new to me. Wish me luck."

Treat

End the conversation with a statement
Example: "Bye now."

Complete task now!

Laundromat
MeNu template

(Complete task template by recounting the social dialogue used in task activity)

Starter
(Write in the starter you used in this task)

_____

_____

_____

Main course
(Write in the main course you used in this task)

_____

_____

_____

_____

_____

Treat
(Write in the treat you used in this task)

_____

_____

_____

Laundromat
Checklist

Please answer each of the following checklist questions.

Did you complete the task set-up? ☐

Did you complete the task? ☐

Did you accomplish the social goal? ☐

Laundromat
Student feedback questionnaire

Answer each of the following questions and explain each answer.

What was the goal of this task?

_____

_____

_____

How difficult was this task?

_____

_____

_____

Were there any social challenges?

_____

_____

_____

What did you learn?

_____

_____

_____

Could you perform this task independently next time?

_____

_____

_____

When will you perform this task again?

_____

_____

_____

How would you prepare?

_____

_____

_____

Do you have any thoughts, concerns, or questions about this task?

_____

_____

_____

Other laundry or household skill tasks

Complete each of the following tasks independently:

- Use washer and dryer (in home).
- Iron clothes.
- Make bed.
- Vacuum and/or sweep floors.
- Dust furniture.
- Clean bathrooms (tub, toilet, sink, floor, mirror).
- Water indoor potted plants.
- Empty trash.
- Feed pet.

Wash vehicle
Outside home skill

Task: Wash vehicle using soap and water. Vacuum interior and wash windows with window cleaner.

Task set-up: Prepare to wash vehicle by collecting the following: a large bucket, liquid soap (most liquid hand dishwashing soap is fine to use), clean cloth rags or paper towels, water hose (long enough to reach both ends of your vehicle), window cleaner (e.g. Windex). Fill bucket with cold or warm water. Add two tablespoons of dish soap into bucket and mix. Using clean rag, wash and rinse the front section of the vehicle. Do the same for each side, hood, back, and wheels of the vehicle. After washing and rinsing all areas of the vehicle, dry the entire vehicle using a clean dry rag (or paper towels). Vacuum inside of vehicle using a handheld vacuum. Wash windows using window cleaner.

Note: Before washing any vehicle, make sure your vehicle is parked near a water faucet (to attach a water hose) and an outlet (to plug in a vacuum cord). Hint: soap up and wash one section of your vehicle at a time before rinsing with water immediately. Wash windows last.

Social goal: Borrow a water hose from a neighbor to rinse vehicle.

Food for thought

Think of the MeNu as a social reference on how to:

Starter

Start a conversation with an introduction statement
Example: "Hi, I'm Pete from across the street."

Main course

Convey the purpose of your conversation with a statement and/or question
Example: "I was wondering if you had a water hose I could borrow. I'm about to wash my car and realized I don't have a usable water hose. I'll have it back to you within an hour."

Treat

End the conversation with a statement
Example: "Thanks so much."

Complete task now!

Wash vehicle
MeNu template

(Complete task template by recounting the social dialogue used in task activity)

Starter
(Write in the starter you used in this task)

_____

_____

_____

Main course
(Write in the main course you used in this task)

_____

_____

_____

_____

_____

Treat
(Write in the treat you used in this task)

_____

_____

_____

Wash vehicle
Checklist

Please answer each of the following checklist questions.

Did you complete the task set-up? ☐

Did you complete the task? ☐

Did you accomplish the social goal? ☐

Wash vehicle
Student feedback questionnaire

Answer each of the following questions and explain each answer.

What was the goal of this task?

_____

_____

_____

How difficult was this task?

_____

_____

_____

Were there any social challenges?

_____

_____

_____

What did you learn?

_____

_____

_____

Could you perform this task independently next time?

_____

_____

_____

When will you perform this task again?

_____

_____

_____

How would you prepare?

_____

_____

_____

Do you have any thoughts, concerns, or questions about this task?

_____

_____

_____

Other outside home skill tasks

Complete each of the following tasks independently:

- Cut lawn using lawnmower.
- Trim shrubs.
- Water outside potted plants.
- Rake leaves.
- Sweep driveway or shovel driveway.
- Clean garage.

Change smoke detector batteries
Home repair skill

Task: Remove old batteries from ceiling smoke detector (alarm) and replace with new batteries.

Task set-up: Prepare to replace old batteries with new batteries. Have new batteries, Phillips screwdriver, and stepladder. To remove smoke detector from ceiling, use a secure stepladder to retrieve it. Remove old batteries from the smoke detector and replace with new ones.

Note: Before removing smoke detector, make sure you have the correct size battery (or multiple size batteries to choose from). You will probably need to use a Phillips screwdriver to remove (and then replace) the smoke detector from the ceiling.

Social goal: Ask a relative, friend, or neighbor to assist you in this task.

Food for thought

Think of the MeNu as a social reference on how to:

Starter

Start a conversation with an introduction statement
Example: "Hi, I'm Linda from next door."

Main course

Convey the purpose of your conversation with a statement and/or question
Example: "I was wondering if you had a ladder I could borrow. I'm changing the batteries for all the smoke detectors in my house."

Treat

End the conversation with a statement
Example: "Thanks so much."

Complete task now!

Change smoke detector batteries
MeNu template

(Complete task template by recounting the social dialogue used in task activity)

Starter

(Write in the starter you used in this task)

_____

_____

_____

Main course

(Write in the main course you used in this task)

_____

_____

_____

_____

_____

Treat

(Write in the treat you used in this task)

_____

_____

_____

Change smoke detector batteries
Checklist

Please answer each of the following checklist questions.

Did you complete the task set-up? ☐

Did you complete the task? ☐

Did you accomplish the social goal? ☐

Change smoke detector batteries
Student feedback questionnaire

Answer each of the following questions and explain each answer.

What was the goal of this task?

_____

_____

_____

How difficult was this task?

_____

_____

_____

Were there any social challenges?

_____

_____

_____

What did you learn?

_____

_____

_____

Could you perform this task independently next time?

_____

_____

_____

When will you perform this task again?

_____

_____

_____

How would you prepare?

_____

_____

_____

Do you have any thoughts, concerns, or questions about this task?

_____

_____

_____

Other home repair skill tasks

Complete each of the following tasks independently:

- Change old light bulbs with new ones in lamps or lighting fixtures. Important warning: To do this safely you *must* first unplug lamp from wall socket and/or turn off power to lighting fixture.
- Plunge toilet when it overflows. (Turn water valve off behind toilet before plunging.)
- Climb ladder to change a light bulb.
- Use hammer, screwdriver and nails to hang a picture on the wall.
- Patch or paint a wall.

Public transportation ticket purchase
Community skill

Task: Purchase a public transit bus ticket independently.

Task set-up: Contact your public information service, reference the local telephone directory, and search the internet for information regarding public bus transportation available in your area, such as bus schedules, fees, and bus locations.

Note: Public transportation is available in most cities and available to the general public.

Social goal: Interact with a passenger on the bus (e.g. for directions, arrival time, fee).

Food for thought

Think of the MeNu as a social reference on how to:

Starter

Start a conversation with an introduction statement
Example: "Hi, I have a question."

Main course

Convey the purpose of your conversation with a statement and/or question
Example: "I'd like to take the bus downtown. Do you know where I can purchase a bus ticket?"

Treat

End the conversation with a statement
Example: "Thanks so much for your help."

Complete task now!

Public transportation ticket purchase
MeNu template

(Complete task template by recounting the social dialogue used in task activity)

Starter
(Write in the starter you used in this task)

_____

_____

_____

Main course
(Write in the main course you used in this task)

_____

_____

_____

_____

_____

Treat
(Write in the treat you used in this task)

_____

_____

_____

Public transportation ticket purchase
Checklist

Please answer each of the following checklist questions.

Did you complete the task set-up? ☐

Did you complete the task? ☐

Did you accomplish the social goal? ☐

Public transportation ticket purchase
Student feedback questionnaire

Answer each of the following questions and explain each answer.

What was the goal of this task?

_____

_____

_____

How difficult was this task?

_____

_____

_____

Were there any social challenges?

_____

_____

_____

What did you learn?

_____

_____

_____

Could you perform this task independently next time?

_____

_____

_____

When will you perform this task again?

_____

_____

_____

How would you prepare?

_____

_____

_____

Do you have any thoughts, concerns, or questions about this task?

_____

_____

_____

Library book return
Community skill

Task: Return library book that is past its due date to public library.

Task set-up: Visit your local library to familiarize yourself with the location and hours of operation. Search the internet for information regarding how to utilize the library in your area such as how to apply for a library card or the length of time a book may be checked out. You must apply for a library card to check out any library item.

Note: Most cities have a public library, each having their own criteria for lending books and other library items.

Social goal: Interact with the librarian to return a library book that is past its due date.

Food for thought

Think of the MeNu as a social reference on how to:

Starter

Start a conversation with an introduction statement
Example: "Hi, my name is John Marco and I need some assistance."

Main course

Convey the purpose of your conversation with a statement and/or question
Example: "I'm here to return a book that is past its due date. Is there a late fee? If so, who here can help me with that? How much is the late fee? Can I write a check?"

Treat

End the conversation with a statement
Example: "Thanks so much for your help."

Complete task now!

Library book return
MeNu template

(Complete task template by recounting the social dialogue used in task activity)

Starter

(Write in the starter you used in this task)

_____

_____

_____

Main course

(Write in the main course you used in this task)

_____

_____

_____

_____

_____

Treat

(Write in the treat you used in this task)

_____

_____

_____

Library book return
Checklist

Please answer each of the following checklist questions.

Did you complete the task set-up? ☐

Did you complete the task? ☐

Did you accomplish the social goal? ☐

Library book return
Student feedback questionnaire

Answer each of the following questions and explain each answer.

What was the goal of this task?

_____

_____

_____

How difficult was this task?

_____

_____

_____

Were there any social challenges?

_____

_____

_____

What did you learn?

_____

_____

_____

Could you perform this task independently next time?

_____

_____

_____

When will you perform this task again?

_____

_____

_____

How would you prepare?

_____

_____

_____

Do you have any thoughts, concerns, or questions about this task?

_____

_____

_____

Other community skill tasks

Complete each of the following tasks independently:

- Use public transport. Purchase a transport ticket for:
    - Subway/Underground
    - Train
    - Plane.
- Schedule air travel reservations.
- Schedule hotel reservations.
- Call a taxi service.
- Drive a vehicle.
- Be aware of pedestrian rules and traffic procedures.
- Use a pay phone.

- Use a map to locate a local park, store, or library.
- Use a GPS to navigate as a passenger in a car.
- Participate in or attend the following:
  - Movies
  - Live theater or playhouse
  - Recreational parks
  - Clubs (e.g. Boy/Girl Scouts, YMCA, swim club)
  - Museum
  - Restaurants
  - Book store
  - Shopping
  - Sporting activities
  - Community pool
  - Health club
  - Video arcades
  - Music concerts
  - Art events
  - Peer camping
  - Family barbecues
  - Summer team activities (e.g. swim team, volleyball, baseball)
  - Winter group trips (e.g. sledding, snowboarding, ice skating).

Restaurant reservation
Social skill

Task: Make a dinner reservation at a local restaurant for you and a friend.

Task set-up: Visit several local restaurants in your area to familiarize yourself with their location and their menu selection. Many restaurants have websites with their menu selection online for patrons to review. Try and select a restaurant that most appeals to you and your dining partner.

Note: Most restaurants require reservations. This is to ensure that the restaurant can accommodate your dining needs, such as the time, date, and size of your dining party. Dining reservations are typically made *prior* to the date you will be dining. If you have specific dietary needs, contact the restaurant in advance to see if they can accommodate you.

Social goal: Interact with the restaurant host or hostess when making the reservation.

Food for thought

Think of the MeNu as a social reference on how to:

Starter

Start a conversation with an introduction statement
Example: "Hello, my name is Betty Paris."

Main course

Convey the purpose of your conversation with a statement and/or question
Example: "I would like to make a dinner reservation for two people, tomorrow night at 7.30 under the name Ms. Paris. Is that possible?"

Treat

End the conversation with a statement
Example: "I appreciate your assistance, thank you."

Complete task now!

Restaurant reservation
MeNu template

(Complete task template by recounting the social dialogue used in task activity)

Starter

(Write in the starter you used in this task)

_____

_____

_____

Main course

(Write in the main course you used in this task)

_____

_____

_____

_____

_____

Treat

(Write in the treat you used in this task)

_____

_____

_____

Restaurant reservation
Checklist

Please answer each of the following checklist questions.

Did you complete the task set-up? ☐

Did you complete the task? ☐

Did you accomplish the social goal? ☐

Restaurant reservation
Student feedback questionnaire

Answer each of the following questions and explain each answer.

What was the goal of this task?

_____

_____

_____

How difficult was this task?

_____

_____

_____

Were there any social challenges?

_____

_____

_____

What did you learn?

_____

_____

_____

Could you perform this task independently next time?

_____

_____

_____

When will you perform this task again?

_____

_____

_____

How would you prepare?

_____

_____

_____

Do you have any thoughts, concerns, or questions about this task?

_____

_____

_____

Restaurant dining conversation
Social skill

Task: Share a conversation "on topic" with your dining partner while dining out.

Task set-up: Review Chapter 2 "Topic planning MeNu principles" and Chapter 5 "Chomping at the tidbits." Select subject topics that are of common interest to you and your dining partner to discuss while dining.

Note: Casual conversation often occurs between people who are dining together. Below is a "Food for thought" reference example for social dining conversation. Practice dialoguing prior to your outing.

Social goal: Share an interactive social conversation with your dining partner.

Food for thought

Think of the MeNu as a social reference on how to:

Starter

Start a conversation with an introduction statement
Example: "Hi, how are you? I'm starving. Are you hungry?"

Main course

Convey the purpose of your conversation with a statement and/or question
Example: "I'm glad we could meet up tonight. There's a school football game Friday night. Want to go with me?"

Treat

End the conversation with a statement
Example: "It was great to see you. Thanks for meeting me for dinner."

Complete task now!

Restaurant dining conversation
MeNu template

(Complete task template by recounting the social dialogue used in task activity)

Starter

(Write in the starter you used in this task)

_____

_____

_____

Main course

(Write in the main course you used in this task)

_____

_____

_____

_____

_____

Treat

(Write in the treat you used in this task)

_____

_____

_____

Restaurant dining conversation
Checklist

Please answer each of the following checklist questions.

Did you complete the task set-up? ☐

Did you complete the task? ☐

Did you accomplish the social goal? ☐

Restaurant dining conversation
Student feedback questionnaire

Answer each of the following questions and explain each answer.

What was the goal of this task?

_____

_____

_____

How difficult was this task?

_____

_____

_____

Were there any social challenges?

_____

_____

_____

What did you learn?

_____

_____

_____

Could you perform this task independently next time?

_____

_____

_____

When will you perform this task again?

_____

_____

_____

How would you prepare?

_____

_____

_____

Do you have any thoughts, concerns, or questions about this task?

_____

_____

_____

Other social skill tasks

Complete each of the following tasks independently:
- Attend a birthday gathering for friend or relative.
- Attend a holiday party for students, co-workers, or friends.
- Attend a family event such as a family reunion or summer weekend trip.
- Invite a friend over for a pizza and video party.
- Invite friends over to play group games such as poker, board games, or basic card games.
- Join a community club, church group, support group, or health club.
- Join a team sport such as basketball or volleyball.
- Organize a party or event for two classmates such as bowling or a movie.
- Be in charge of planning your family vacation either locally or internationally.

- Plan an overnight outing with a peer or club group such as camping, skiing, or rock climbing.
- Join a community theater group.
- Join a religious school peer group.
- Try out for a school group such as student council or cheerleading.
- Attend a school football game or dance.
- Invite a date to your formal dance.
- Invite some friends or family to your graduation ceremony.
- Join an after-school club such as art, track, or a computer media class.
- Attend a weekend school event such as a dance, basketball game, or soccer game.
- Participate in a school fundraising activity such as a car wash or bake sale.

MeNu options discussion questions

Review each question with your instructor.

- Which life skill task was most challenging? Why?

_____

_____

_____

- Which life skill task was the least challenging? Why?

_____

_____

_____

- Do you feel that you have good problem-solving skills? Give an example.

_____

_____

_____

- What life skill task created the most social anxiety for you? Explain.

_____

_____

_____

- Based on your task experiences in Chapter 6, how would you prepare yourself in the future?

_____

_____

_____

- Give an example of why effective social skills are important when interacting with people in the community? Explain.

_____

_____

_____

- How are social skills and life skills related? Give an example.

  _____

  _____

  _____

- What's your best social skill? Give an example.

  _____

  _____

  _____

- What's your best life skill? Give an example.

  _____

  _____

  _____

- Is there an area you feel you could improve? Explain.

  _____

  _____

  _____

- What did you learn most about yourself from the independent life skills tasks in Chapter 6? Explain.

  _____

  _____

  _____

- If you could live independently tomorrow, what are the five most important *social* skills you'd need to be proficient in to be successful?

  _____

  _____

  _____

- If you could live independently tomorrow, what are the five most important *life* skills you'd need to be proficient in to be successful?

_____

_____

_____

- Do you want to live independently? Why or why not?

_____

_____

_____

Chapter 6 summary

In this chapter students integrated social skill MeNu techniques and strategies, outlined in Chapters 1 through 5, with real life skill experiences. *The Social and Life Skills MeNu* templates were designed for students to acquire the skill set to practice their social communications effectively and appropriately with others while simultaneously developing their daily life skills in the community.

Goal

Students participated in social outings to broaden their social experiences.

Objective

To achieve independence by enhancing social interactions while improving life skill abilities in the community.

MeNu Templates

List of templates

- Refill pharmacy prescription
- Shop for own clothing
- Use telephone book and internet as resources
- Class school project
- Pay with a check to purchase item from store
- Bake cookies following a recipe
- Turn off main gas line in an emergency
- Empty trash on garbage collection day
- Sweep or shovel snow from driveway
- Change light bulbs
- Air travel ticket purchase
- Movie and dinner date
- Blank template

Refill pharmacy prescription
Self health care skill

Task: _____

_____

Task set-up: _____

_____

_____

_____

Social goal: _____

_____

Food for thought

Think of the MeNu as a social reference on how to:

Starter

Start a conversation with an introduction statement

Example: _____

Main course

Convey the purpose of your conversation with a statement and/or question

Example: _____

_____

Treat

End the conversation with a statement

Example: _____

Refill pharmacy prescription
MeNu template

(Complete task template by recounting the social dialogue used in task activity)

Starter

(Write in the starter you used in this task)

_____

_____

_____

Main course

(Write in the main course you used in this task)

_____

_____

_____

_____

_____

Treat

(Write in the treat you used in this task)

_____

_____

_____

Refill pharmacy prescription
Checklist

Please answer each of the following checklist questions.

Did you complete the task set-up? ☐

Did you complete the task? ☐

Did you accomplish the social goal? ☐

Refill pharmacy prescription
Student feedback questionnaire

Answer each of the following questions and explain each answer.

What was the goal of this task?

_____

_____

_____

How difficult was this task?

_____

_____

_____

Were there any social challenges?

_____

_____

_____

What did you learn?

_____

_____

_____

Could you perform this task independently next time?

_____

_____

_____

When will you perform this task again?

_____

_____

_____

How would you prepare?

_____

_____

_____

Do you have any thoughts, concerns, or questions about this task?

_____

_____

_____

Shop for own clothing
Personal skill

Task: _____

_____

Task set-up: _____

_____

_____

_____

Social goal: _____

_____

Food for thought

Think of the MeNu as a social reference on how to:

Starter

Start a conversation with an introduction statement

Example: _____

Main course

Convey the purpose of your conversation with a statement and/or question

Example: _____

_____

Treat

End the conversation with a statement

Example: _____

Shop for own clothing
MeNu template

(Complete task template by recounting the social dialogue used in task activity)

Starter

(Write in the starter you used in this task)

_____

_____

_____

Main course

(Write in the main course you used in this task)

_____

_____

_____

_____

_____

Treat

(Write in the treat you used in this task)

_____

_____

_____

Shop for own clothing
Checklist

Please answer each of the following checklist questions.

Did you complete the task set-up? ☐

Did you complete the task? ☐

Did you accomplish the social goal? ☐

Shop for own clothing
Student feedback questionnaire

Answer each of the following questions and explain each answer:

What was the goal of this task?

_____

_____

_____

How difficult was this task?

_____

_____

_____

Were there any social challenges?

_____

_____

_____

What did you learn?

_____

_____

_____

Could you perform this task independently next time?

_____

_____

_____

When will you perform this task again?

_____

_____

_____

How would you prepare?

_____

_____

_____

Do you have any thoughts, concerns, or questions about this task?

_____

_____

_____

Use telephone book and internet as resources
Basic information skill

Task: _____

_____

Task set-up: _____

_____

_____

_____

Social goal: _____

_____

Food for thought

Think of the MeNu as a social reference on how to:

Starter

Start a conversation with an introduction statement

Example: _____

Main course

Convey the purpose of your conversation with a statement and/or question

Example: _____

_____

Treat

End the conversation with a statement

Example: _____

Use telephone book and internet as resources
MeNu template

(Complete task template by recounting the social dialogue used in task activity)

Starter

(Write in the starter you used in this task)

_____

_____

_____

Main course

(Write in the main course you used in this task)

_____

_____

_____

_____

_____

Treat

(Write in the treat you used in this task)

_____

_____

_____

Use telephone book and internet as resources
Checklist

Please answer each of the following checklist questions.

Did you complete the task set-up? ☐

Did you complete the task? ☐

Did you accomplish the social goal? ☐

Use telephone book and internet as resources
Student feedback questionnaire

Answer each of the following questions and explain each answer.

What was the goal of this task?

_____

_____

_____

How difficult was this task?

_____

_____

_____

Were there any social challenges?

_____

_____

_____

What did you learn?

_____

_____

_____

Could you perform this task independently next time?

_____

_____

_____

When will you perform this task again?

_____

_____

_____

How would you prepare?

_____

_____

_____

Do you have any thoughts, concerns, or questions about this task?

_____

_____

_____

Class school project
Time-management and planning skill

Task: _____

_____

Task set-up: _____

_____

_____

_____

Social goal: _____

_____

Food for thought

Think of the MeNu as a social reference on how to:

Starter

Start a conversation with an introduction statement

Example: _____

Main course

Convey the purpose of your conversation with a statement and/or question

Example: _____

_____

Treat

End the conversation with a statement

Example: _____

Class school project
MeNu template

(Complete task template by recounting the social dialogue used in task activity)

Starter

(Write in the starter you used in this task)

_____

_____

_____

Main course

(Write in the main course you used in this task)

_____

_____

_____

_____

_____

Treat

(Write in the treat you used in this task)

_____

_____

_____

Class school project
Checklist

Please answer each of the following checklist questions.

Did you complete the task set-up? ☐

Did you complete the task? ☐

Did you accomplish the social goal? ☐

Class school project
Student feedback questionnaire

Answer each of the following questions and explain each answer.

What was the goal of this task?

_____

_____

_____

How difficult was this task?

_____

_____

_____

Were there any social challenges?

_____

_____

_____

What did you learn?

_____

_____

_____

Could you perform this task independently next time?

_____

_____

_____

When will you perform this task again?

_____

_____

_____

How would you prepare?

_____

_____

_____

Do you have any thoughts, concerns, or questions about this task?

_____

_____

_____

Pay with a check to purchase item from store
Money skill

Task: _____

_____

Task set-up: _____

_____

_____

_____

Social goal: _____

_____

Food for thought

Think of the MeNu as a social reference on how to:

Starter

Start a conversation with an introduction statement

Example: _____

Main course

Convey the purpose of your conversation with a statement and/or question

Example: _____

_____

Treat

End the conversation with a statement

Example: _____

Pay with a check to purchase item from store
MeNu template

(Complete task template by recounting the social dialogue used in task activity)

Starter
(Write in the starter you used in this task)

_____

_____

_____

Main course
(Write in the main course you used in this task)

_____

_____

_____

_____

Treat
(Write in the treat you used in this task)

_____

_____

_____

Pay with a check to purchase item from store
Checklist

Please answer each of the following checklist questions.

Did you complete the task set-up? ☐

Did you complete the task? ☐

Did you accomplish the social goal? ☐

Pay with a check to purchase item from store
Student feedback questionnaire

Answer each of the following questions and explain each answer.

What was the goal of this task?

_____

_____

_____

How difficult was this task?

_____

_____

_____

Were there any social challenges?

_____

_____

_____

What did you learn?

_____

_____

_____

Could you perform this task independently next time?

_____

_____

_____

When will you perform this task again?

_____

_____

_____

How would you prepare?

_____

_____

_____

Do you have any thoughts, concerns, or questions about this task?

_____

_____

_____

Bake cookies following a recipe
Cooking and meal-planning skill

Task: _____

_____

Task set-up: _____

_____

_____

_____

Social goal: _____

_____

Food for thought

Think of the MeNu as a social reference on how to:

Starter

Start a conversation with an introduction statement

Example: _____

Main course

Convey the purpose of your conversation with a statement and/or question

Example: _____

_____

Treat

End the conversation with a statement

Example: _____

Bake cookies following a recipe
MeNu template

(Complete task template by recounting the social dialogue used in task activity)

Starter

(Write in the starter you used in this task)

_____

_____

_____

Main course

(Write in the main course you used in this task)

_____

_____

_____

_____

_____

Treat

(Write in the treat you used in this task)

_____

_____

_____

Bake cookies following a recipe
Checklist

Please answer each of the following checklist questions.

Did you complete the task set-up? ☐

Did you complete the task? ☐

Did you accomplish the social goal? ☐

Bake cookies following a recipe
Student feedback questionnaire

Answer each of the following questions and explain each answer.

What was the goal of this task?

_____

_____

_____

How difficult was this task?

_____

_____

_____

Were there any social challenges?

_____

_____

_____

What did you learn?

_____

_____

_____

Could you perform this task independently next time?

_____

_____

_____

When will you perform this task again?

_____

_____

_____

How would you prepare?

_____

_____

_____

Do you have any thoughts, concerns, or questions about this task?

_____

_____

_____

Turn off main gas line in an emergency
Emergency skill

Task: _____

_____

Task set-up: _____

_____

_____

_____

Social goal: _____

_____

Food for thought

Think of the MeNu as a social reference on how to:

Starter

Start a conversation with an introduction statement

Example: _____

Main course

Convey the purpose of your conversation with a statement and/or question

Example: _____

_____

Treat

End the conversation with a statement

Example: _____

Turn off main gas line in an emergency
MeNu template

(Complete task template by recounting the social dialogue used in task activity)

Starter

(Write in the starter you used in this task)

_____

_____

_____

Main course

(Write in the main course you used in this task)

_____

_____

_____

_____

_____

Treat

(Write in the treat you used in this task)

_____

_____

_____

Turn off main gas line in an emergency
Checklist

Please answer each of the following checklist questions.

Did you complete the task set-up? ☐

Did you complete the task? ☐

Did you accomplish the social goal? ☐

Turn off main gas line in an emergency
Student feedback questionnaire

Answer each of the following questions and explain each answer.

What was the goal of this task?

_____

_____

_____

How difficult was this task?

_____

_____

_____

Were there any social challenges?

_____

_____

_____

What did you learn?

_____

_____

_____

Could you perform this task independently next time?

_____

_____

_____

When will you perform this task again?

_____

_____

_____

How would you prepare?

_____

_____

_____

Do you have any thoughts, concerns, or questions about this task?

_____

_____

_____

Empty trash on garbage collection day
Laundry or household skill

Task: _____

_____

Task set-up: _____

_____

_____

_____

Social goal: _____

_____

Food for thought

Think of the MeNu as a social reference on how to:

Starter

Start a conversation with an introduction statement

Example: _____

Main course

Convey the purpose of your conversation with a statement and/or question

Example: _____

_____

Treat

End the conversation with a statement

Example: _____

Empty trash on garbage collection day
MeNu template

(Complete task template by recounting the social dialogue used in task activity)

Starter
(Write in the starter you used in this task)

_____

_____

_____

Main course
(Write in the main course you used in this task)

_____

_____

_____

_____

_____

Treat
(Write in the treat you used in this task)

_____

_____

_____

Empty trash on garbage collection day
Checklist

Please answer each of the following checklist questions.

Did you complete the task set-up? ☐

Did you complete the task? ☐

Did you accomplish the social goal? ☐

Empty trash on garbage collection day
Student feedback questionnaire

Answer each of the following questions and explain each answer.

What was the goal of this task?

_____

_____

_____

How difficult was this task?

_____

_____

_____

Were there any social challenges?

_____

_____

_____

What did you learn?

_____

_____

_____

Could you perform this task independently next time?

_____

_____

_____

When will you perform this task again?

_____

_____

_____

How would you prepare?

_____

_____

_____

Do you have any thoughts, concerns, or questions about this task?

_____

_____

_____

Sweep or shovel snow from driveway
Outside home skill

Task: _____

_____

Task set-up: _____

_____

_____

_____

Social goal: _____

_____

Food for thought

Think of the MeNu as a social reference on how to:

Starter

Start a conversation with an introduction statement

Example: _____

Main course

Convey the purpose of your conversation with a statement and/or question

Example: _____

_____

Treat

End the conversation with a statement

Example: _____

Sweep or shovel snow from driveway
MeNu template

(Complete task template by recounting the social dialogue used in task activity)

Starter

(Write in the starter you used in this task)

_____

_____

_____

Main course

(Write in the main course you used in this task)

_____

_____

_____

_____

_____

Treat

(Write in the treat you used in this task)

_____

_____

_____

Sweep or shovel snow from driveway
Checklist

Please answer each of the following checklist questions.

Did you complete the task set-up? ☐

Did you complete the task? ☐

Did you accomplish the social goal? ☐

Sweep or shovel snow from driveway
Student feedback questionnaire

Answer each of the following questions and explain each answer.

What was the goal of this task?

_____

_____

_____

How difficult was this task?

_____

_____

_____

Were there any social challenges?

_____

_____

_____

What did you learn?

_____

_____

_____

Could you perform this task independently next time?

_____

_____

_____

When will you perform this task again?

_____

_____

_____

How would you prepare?

_____

_____

_____

Do you have any thoughts, concerns, or questions about this task?

_____

_____

_____

Change light bulbs
Home repair skill

Task: _____

_____

Task set-up: _____

_____

_____

_____

Social goal: _____

_____

Food for thought

Think of the MeNu as a social reference on how to:

Starter

Start a conversation with an introduction statement

Example: _____

Main course

Convey the purpose of your conversation with a statement and/or question

Example: _____

_____

Treat

End the conversation with a statement

Example: _____

Change light bulb
MeNu template

(Complete task template by r   ing the social dialogue used in task activity)

Starter
(Write in the starter you   n this task)

_____   _____

_____   _____

_____   _____

Main course
(Write in the r   ourse you used in this task)

_____   _____

_____   _____

_____   _____

_____   _____

_____   _____

Tr
(e in the treat you used in this task)

_____   _____

_____   _____

_____   _____

Change light bulbs
Checklist

Please answer each of the following checklist questions.

Did you complete the task set-up? ☐

Did you complete the task? ☐

Did you accomplish the social goal? ☐

Change light bulbs
Student feedback questionnaire

Answer each of the following questions and explain each answer.

What was the goal of this task?

_____

_____

_____

How difficult was this task?

_____

_____

_____

Were there any social challenges?

_____

_____

_____

What did you learn?

_____

_____

_____

Could you perform this task independently next time?

_____

_____

_____

When will you perform this task again?

_____

_____

_____

How would you prepare?

_____

_____

_____

Do you have any thoughts, concerns, or questions about this task?

_____

_____

_____

Air travel ticket purchase
Community skill

Task: _____

_____

Task set-up: _____

_____

_____

_____

Social goal: _____

_____

Food for thought

Think of the MeNu as a social reference on how to:

Starter

Start a conversation with an introduction statement

Example: _____

Main course

Convey the purpose of your conversation with a statement and/or question

Example: _____

_____

Treat

End the conversation with a statement

Example: _____

Air travel ticket purchase
MeNu template

(Complete task template by recounting the social dialogue used in task activity)

Starter
(Write in the starter you used in this task)

_____

_____

_____

Main course
(Write in the main course you used in this task)

_____

_____

_____

_____

_____

Treat
(Write in the treat you used in this task)

_____

_____

_____

Air travel ticket purchase
Checklist

Please answer each of the following checklist questions.

Did you complete the task set-up? ☐

Did you complete the task? ☐

Did you accomplish the social goal? ☐

Air travel ticket purchase
Student feedback questionnaire

Answer each of the following questions and explain each answer.

What was the goal of this task?

_____

_____

_____

How difficult was this task?

_____

_____

_____

Were there any social challenges?

_____

_____

_____

What did you learn?

_____

_____

_____

Could you perform this task independently next time?

_____

_____

_____

When will you perform this task again?

_____

_____

_____

How would you prepare?

_____

_____

_____

Do you have any thoughts, concerns, or questions about this task?

_____

_____

_____

Movie and dinner date
Social skill

Task: _____

_____

Task set-up: _____

_____

_____

_____

Social goal: _____

_____

Food for thought

Think of the MeNu as a social reference on how to:

Starter

Start a conversation with an introduction statement

Example: _____

Main course

Convey the purpose of your conversation with a statement and/or question

Example: _____

_____

Treat

End the conversation with a statement

Example: _____

Movie and dinner date
MeNu template

(Complete task template by recounting the social dialogue used in task activity)

Starter

(Write in the starter you used in this task)

_____

_____

_____

Main course

(Write in the main course you used in this task)

_____

_____

_____

_____

Treat

(Write in the treat you used in this task)

_____

_____

_____

Movie and dinner date
Checklist

Please answer each of the following checklist questions.

Did you complete the task set-up? ☐

Did you complete the task? ☐

Did you accomplish the social goal? ☐

Movie and dinner date
Student feedback questionnaire

Answer each of the following questions and explain each answer.

What was the goal of this task?

_____

_____

_____

How difficult was this task?

_____

_____

_____

Were there any social challenges?

_____

_____

_____

What did you learn?

_____

_____

_____

Could you perform this task independently next time?

_____

_____

_____

When will you perform this task again?

_____

_____

_____

How would you prepare?

_____

_____

_____

Do you have any thoughts, concerns, or questions about this task?

_____

_____

_____

Task:
Skill:

Task: _____

_____

Task set-up: _____

_____

_____

_____

Social goal: _____

_____

Food for thought

Think of the MeNu as a social reference on how to:

Starter

Start a conversation with an introduction statement

_____

_____

Main course

Convey the purpose of your conversation with a statement and/or question

_____

_____

_____

Treat

End the conversation with a statement

_____

_____

Task:
MeNu template

(Complete task template by recounting the social dialogue used in task activity)

Starter
(Write in the starter you used in this task)

_____

_____

_____

Main course
(Write in the main course you used in this task)

_____

_____

_____

_____

_____

Treat
(Write in the treat you used in this task)

_____

_____

_____

Task:
Checklist

Please answer each of the following checklist questions.

Did you complete the task set-up? ☐

Did you complete the task? ☐

Did you accomplish the social goal? ☐

Task:
Student feedback questionnaire

Answer each of the following questions and explain each answer.

What was the goal of this task?

_____

_____

_____

How difficult was this task?

_____

_____

_____

Were there any social challenges?

_____

_____

_____

What did you learn?

_____

_____

_____

Could you perform this task independently next time?

_____

_____

_____

When will you perform this task again?

_____

_____

_____

How would you prepare?

_____

_____

_____

Do you have any thoughts, concerns, or questions about this task?

_____

_____

_____

Resources

Tony Attwood

www.tonyattwood.com.au—A guide for parents, professionals, and people with Asperger's syndrome and their partners.

Karra M. Barber

www.aspergersresource.org—Information about Asperger's syndrome and other autism spectrum disorders, including resources and educational materials, transition tricks and tips, and support agencies.

Michelle Garcia Winner

www.socialthinking.com—Website devoted to social thinking for individuals with autism spectrum disorders.

OASIS@MAAP

www.aspergersyndrome.org—Online Asperger's information and support centre.

Orion Academy

www.orionacademy.org—Orion Academy is a quality college-preparatory program for secondary students whose academic success is compromised by a neurocognitive disability such as Asperger's syndrome or Nonverbal Learning Disorder (NLD). Orion is dedicated to educating students with neurocognitive disorders, targeting both individual social needs and academic excellence.

The UC Davis MIND Institute

www.ucdm.ucdavis.edu/mindinstitute—MIND (Medical Investigation of Neurodevelopmental Disorders) is a collaborative international research center, committed to the awareness, understanding, prevention, care, and cure of neurodevelopmental disorders.

Printed in Great Britain
by Amazon